Hannah Snell

James Wardell Pinx.ᵗ

John Johnson fecit.

Mʳˢ Hannah Snell

Who entered herself as a MARINE in COL. FRASER's Regiment by the name of JAMES GRAY Novemʳ 27.1745.

And went with Admiral Boscawen's Squadron to the East Indies where at the attack of Pondicherry in Septʳ 1748. She received 12 Wounds one of which she cured herself to prevent the discovery of her Sex and after having been 5 Years in the Service was discharg'd June 9ᵗʰ 1750. But upon her Petitioning His Royal Highness the DUKE he was pleas'd to order her a Pension of L30 Pʳ Annum as a Reward for the many signal Services she did her Country in that Expedition.

Printed for & Sold by T. Jefferys at the Corner of Sᵗ Martins Lane Charing Cross

Hannah Snell

THE SECRET LIFE OF A FEMALE MARINE, 1723-1792

MATTHEW STEPHENS

Ship Street Press • London

First published in 1997 by
Ship Street Press
67 Laurel Manor, Devonshire Road,
Sutton, Surrey, SM2 5EJ, England.

42 Merton Street,
Rozelle, NSW, 2039, Australia

ISBN 0-9530565-0-3

Typeset and printed in Australia by
Standard Publishing House Pty Ltd,
69 Nelson St., Rozelle, 2039.

Contents

Acknowledgments		6
Foreword		7
Introduction		9
1	Worcester	12
2	The Call of the City	15
3	Rebellion	18
4	A Passage to India	22
5	The Siege of Pondicherry	25
6	The Mystery of Hannah's Wounds	29
7	Homeward Bound	34
8	Fame	37
9	A Question of Money	44
10	Where do Retired Female Soldiers Go?	47
11	Who was James Gray?	53
Afterword		56
Notes		58

Acknowledgments

The illustrations in this booklet are reproduced by kind permission of the following: frontispiece, © British Museum; pages 14 (Rare Books and Special Collections), 16, 19, 24, 35, 45, 52, General Reference Library, State Library of NSW; page 20, Rector of St. George-in-the-East, Middlesex; page 26, from H.W. Richmond's *The Navy in the War of 1739-48*, Cambridge University Press, 1920, C.U.P.; page 32 [ADM 36/1033], Controller of Her Majesty's Stationery Office; pages 10 and 40, Royal Marines Museum; page 42, Hereford and Worcester County Libraries; page 48, Berkshire Record Office.

I am eternally grateful to Jean and Bill Ryles, whose research skills have enabled me to delve much deeper into Hannah's life than would have been otherwise possible, and I have been privileged to be part of a friendship that has been one of this project's greatest rewards. To those who have worked with me on this booklet, thank you: my partner James Renwick, Dr Sylvia Martin, and Professor John Stephens. I would also like to thank those people who have contributed in a variety of ways: Angela Brooks, Rod Cameron, Susan Campbell, Sophie Cunningham, Margaret Gibbs, Brooke Green, Caroline Kershaw, Matthew Little, Laurie Martin, Irving Martin, Lizzie Mulder, Neal Peres da Costa, Manoa Renwick, and Daniel Yeadon. I am indebted to the librarians and staff at the following institutions: Berkshire CRO, Bethlem Royal Hospital Archives, The British Library, The British Museum, Guildhall Library, India Office Library, London Metropolitan Archives, Middlesex CRO, National Army Museum, National Maritime Museum, The National Trust, Public Record Office, Royal Archives, Royal Chelsea Hospital, Royal Marines Museum, State Library of NSW, Sydney University Library, and Worcestershire CRO. Finally, thank you to those among my family and friends who have supported me throughout this project.

I dedicate this booklet to the memory of my grandfather, Irving George Martin.

Foreword

In March, 1995, I received some amazing news. I was informed by an Australian researcher, Matthew Stephens, that my fifth-generation grandmother was the famous female soldier, Hannah Snell.

I had also been studying my family history, but, as I had been concentrating on the male line, I had not realised the significance of the woman sitting at the top of my family tree. Matthew had made the connection between my family and Hannah after consulting the records of the Church of Jesus Christ of Latter-day Saints, where my family details had been entered some years earlier by my cousin, Anne Bradshaw.

Anne put Matthew in contact with me and I soon learnt that the British Library held a copy of Hannah's biography, published in 1750. We continued our correspondence and from then on developed a long-distance research partnership.

I had been so surprised and excited at the possibility of being related to someone famous that I thought it would probably prove to be a mistake. However, it was true and in August 1995 Matthew came to England to complete his research.

Matthew's wonderful enthusiasm to search out the truth about Hannah brought us all together in a friendship that my husband, Bill, and I will always treasure. His dedication to research has inspired me to keep believing that the facts are there to be found, and that another story about Hannah must not be written using only secondary sources, as so many people have done since 1750. I have read many articles and stories about Hannah and most just quote from the original biography.

This book is a credit to Matthew's dedication and longing to find the truth. I know he has inspired me to carry on searching as long as I am able. I am sure, as I know Matthew is, that this is not the end of the search for Hannah's story and that people will continue talking about her for many years to come.

Jean Ryles
London, 1997

Introduction

On 8 February 1792, Hannah Snell, one of Britain's best-known female soldiers, died in the notorious lunatic asylum, Bedlam. Five months earlier, a newspaper had reported on her deteriorating condition:

> This veteran heroine, who distinguished herself very highly many years ago, by repeated acts of valour, and who served in the navy under the virile habit, is still alive; but it is with regret we inform our readers that she was last week admitted into Bethlehem Hospital, being at present a victim of the most deplorable infirmity that can afflict human nature.[1]

The illness that sent Hannah to Bedlam is unknown, but it was a sad end to the life of a woman who had once strutted the London stage dressed as a marine, thrilling audiences with her adventures on the battlefield.

The story Hannah told her audience was truly extraordinary. She claimed that in 1745, at the age of twenty-two, she was abandoned by her husband while seven months pregnant with their first child. After the baby's premature death she decided to pursue her deceitful lover, disguising herself as her brother-in-law, James Gray, to make her journey safer. A victim of her success at masquerade, Hannah says she was pressed into the English army and forced to march in pursuit of the fleeing troops of Bonnie Prince Charlie. She then joined the marines and was sent to India, where she fought against the French at Pondicherry. She claims to have been severely injured there, but managed to conceal her sex by treating her wounds in secret. After a further ten months of service, she returned home with the rest of the fleet in late 1749.

After four and a half years of dressing as a man, she arrived back in London and quickly revealed her secret to an excited public. She presented a petition to the head of the British army, the Duke of Cumberland, requesting financial recognition for her service. While the military was examining the truth of her claims, Hannah became the toast of London - her story was a best seller and her portrait was sold on every street corner. Finally, the army accepted Hannah's version of events and she was granted a lifelong pension. By the end of 1750, word of this twenty-seven-year-old's adventures had spread across the whole of Britain.

For over two centuries, people have been fascinated by Hannah's life, and her story has appeared in a great variety of forms, including newspaper articles, biographies, a Prime Ministerial speech and even a rock opera. Yet despite all this attention, much of this extraordinary woman's life remains a mystery. Hannah's shadowy history is an inevitable result of her lowly beginnings. There is no grand house bursting with family papers, no ancient family tree with a royal lineage - instead we are left with the musters of common soldiers and a scattering of records tracing the everyday lives of labourers, shopkeepers and servants. In addition to these simple sources, however, is a document that has proved invaluable in recreating Hannah's life. In June 1750, the printer and publisher Robert Walker made an agreement with Hannah to publish her biography, *The Female Soldier; or The Surprising Life and Adventures of Hannah Snell.*[2] The book was a runaway success and Walker published a much longer, serialised edition barely a fortnight later, ensuring Hannah's place in history.

The retelling of Hannah's story has been subject to many inaccuracies. While our contemporaries can challenge such defamation through the courts, historical figures have no recourse against the misinformation propagated by succeeding generations. The inconsistent treatment of Hannah's story, while perhaps not malicious, reflects an age when biographers were little concerned with establishing a factually based "truth". The original biography by Robert Walker has been used by many writers as their only source of information. Inevitably some of these have misreported the story and their errors have been copied by others at a later date. Like an ancient game of Chinese whispers, the tale has become riddled with mistakes and misinterpretation. After reading many of these

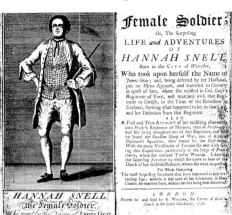

The second edition of Walker's biography.

10

different versions, the student of Hannah's life is left utterly confused as to where the truth really lies.

A reappraisal of all the surviving material relating to Hannah's life is clearly long overdue. I will challenge most of the secondary treatments of Hannah's tale by testing Walker's biography against the primary sources. The most common error made by the majority of commentators has been in their reading of this original biography. Whereas some have dismissed it as utter fiction, others have taken every word as gospel.

The greatest challenge for anyone exploring Hannah's life is to discover whether the celebrity appearing on stage under the name of Hannah Snell was actually the same individual who went by the name of James Gray in India. Not one eighteenth-century account questions Hannah's honesty. However, less than a decade into the 1800s, commentators were beginning to raise doubts about her story and by the early 1890s the periodical *Notes and Queries* had printed a series of letters debating the veracity of her adventures.[3] Now I hope to join the debate armed with new evidence that will take us a step closer to validating, or disproving, Hannah's claims.

The tradition of the female soldier was already well-established by the time Hannah began treading the boards in 1750. The stories of these women were a common subject of the ballads of the day. While these songs were particularly popular among the lower classes, Walker's biography is considered significant because it is actually directed towards wealthier, novel-buying readers.[4] The notion of disguise would not have been foreign to this new audience, as it was common for Londoners during this period to attend the many masquerade balls held at pleasure gardens dotted around the city. Indeed, one of the most popular actresses of the eighteenth century, Peg Woffington, was celebrated for her appearances in male roles. Yet the gritty detail of Hannah's story would have been unfamiliar to this middlebrow audience, and the biography's author battles with this material - even rearranging it - as he tries to present it in a way that makes sense to his readers.

It is inevitable that the exploration of an eighteenth-century life (or any life for that matter) will never be complete - even more so if the subject is impoverished and a woman, let alone a woman whose infamy is based upon her ability to keep a secret. Yet surviving records provide us with a unique opportunity to explore the world of the female cross-dresser in the eighteenth century.

1

Worcester

H annah Snell informed her biographer, Robert Walker, that she was born on 23 April 1723, in Friar Street, in the parish of St. Helen's, Worcester. Two years after her birth, Daniel Defoe wrote:

> Worcester is a large, populous, old, tho' not very well built City; I say not well built because the Town is close and old, the Houses standing too thick. This City is very full of People, and the People generally esteem'd very rich, being full of Business, occasion'd chiefly by the Cloathing Trade, of which the City and the Country round carries on a great share.[1]

Hannah had been born into a thriving community of around 10,000 people. It was a picturesque cathedral city whose proximity to the River Severn ensured a continuing prosperity.

Hunting for evidence of Hannah's early years, I was delighted to discover that her very own parish church, St. Helen's, is now the Worcestershire Record Office. Unfortunately, a quick perusal of the City's records soon left me feeling disappointed. There appeared to be no sign of Hannah's habitation in Worcester - it was almost as if her name had been scrubbed from every possible source and I soon began to wonder whether she had ever existed. Thankfully Hannah gave Walker a detailed description of her family, and further searches revealed a number of documents relating to the Snells that lent credence to her story.

Hannah says she was the eighth of nine children belonging to the hosier and dyer, Samuel Snell, and the grand-daughter of Captain-Lieutenant Samuel Snell, who supposedly died bravely at the Battle of Malplaquet in 1709. While there is no record of this illustrious war hero, marriage records do provide information about his son. Samuel Snell, a dyer, born in 1680, married Elizabeth Marston, the daughter of a shoemaker, in 1702.[2] Sometime during the early 1700s Samuel took over the lease of a Friar Street house, probably number 25, belonging to John Southall in the parish of St. Helen's.[3] Following the death of his first wife, Samuel remarried in 1709 to Mary Williams, a twenty-five-year-old resident of the neighbouring parish of St. Peter's.[4] While it is not known which of the nine children belonged to which wife, it is probable that Hannah was Mary's daughter.

In Walker's biography, we are told that Hannah's bravery was a gift passed down through her father's side of the family. Although Hannah's father had little opportunity to display his supposed gallantry while employed in the textile industry, her grandfather and brother, a foot soldier, are portrayed as heroes. Describing a family of soldiers and sailors of almost regimental proportions, Walker would have us believe that bravery ran thick in the veins of the Snells. His readers may have been a little more sceptical, perhaps suspecting that this was a virtue driven by necessity, where poor economic circumstance left Hannah and her siblings with few other choices.

As a dyer, Samuel Snell had made his living in the textile industry - the linchpin of Worcester's local economy since the sixteenth century. However, at the time of Hannah's birth there were early signs of a downturn in the trade, which, by the 1770s, had been superseded by glove manufacturing.[5] It is possible that this gradual withering of the cloth industry affected the prosperity of Hannah's family. Their position in Worcester society is suggested by Samuel's marriage to the daughter of a shoemaker and the family's residence in Friar Street - traditionally the home of small tradesmen where none of the properties were particularly large.

While living in Friar street, the Snells witnessed a steady decline in the quality of their neighbourhood. In 1724, a house only a few doors down from number 25 was converted into the City Gaol and this must have been of particular concern to the local inhabitants, given the risks of gaol fever. It was also around this time that a number of cottages were built in the rear gardens of many of the properties facing onto Friar Street, making it an even less desirable place to live.

17-25 Friar Street.

If you take a stroll down Friar Street today, you will find a narrow stretch of beautifully renovated Elizabethan shops and houses whose beams have bowed under the weight of the centuries. Numbers 17-25 were built on the site of a medieval Franciscan Friary in the mid-sixteenth century, though evidence of the Tudor construction is now concealed by a Georgian facade. It seems ironic that number 25, the former home of such a famous cross-dresser, should now be occupied by two dress shops.

While it is likely that Hannah had a crowded and relatively tough childhood, her biographer provides us with few details about her life in Worcester. Other than a fanciful anecdote describing Hannah's love of dressing up as a soldier at the age of ten and parading around the town with her friends, the only other information relates to her schooling. Luckier than many girls of the period, she received a rudimentary education, in which she learnt to read, though not to write. This is not surprising, as writing was considered a lower priority than reading for children from poor families. This was even more the case with girls, "whose business is most within doors at home, who may have but very little occasion, and as little inclination to use a pen".[6] Despite Hannah's inability to write, it would be gratifying to think that she was literate enough to read the biography that brought her fame and fortune.

A late eighteenth-century view of Worcester

2

The Call of the City

Robert Walker says that on Christmas Day, 1740, the seventeen-year-old Hannah arrived in London. Both her parents had probably died by this date and there appears to have been no other family members in Worcester in a position to support her. Walker notes with a disarming matter-of-factness that "it is a common Thing to observe a Family dispersed when the Heads of that Family are either laid in their Graves or by accidental Calamities rendered incapable of supporting it longer" (page 16). Hannah was one of many young provincial women at this time travelling to London in the hope of a better life. Her arrival in the capital echoes that of Moll Hackabout, William Hogarth's archetypal innocent entering the lair of the "wicked" city. Unlike Moll, who was to become a victim of the procuress, Mother Needham, and her customers, Hannah handled her own affairs with a self-reliance not often attributed to women of this time.

Hannah quickly settled into the home of her sister and brother-in-law, Susannah and James Gray. Susannah, then thirty-two years old, was probably the daughter of Elizabeth Snell and therefore Hannah's half-sister. James Gray, thirty-seven, was a house carpenter by trade. The couple shared a small house in Ship Street, Wapping - a rough dockside parish, not far from the Tower of London.[1]

The details of how Hannah passed her time in Wapping remain sketchy. There is no doubt that she would have sought employment and was probably expected to make a monetary contribution to the household. Hannah and women like her were faced with few options for economic survival other than work requiring long hours and hard physical labour. In light of Hannah's success at masquerading as a man, one must assume that she was a strong woman and was used to physical work. It is also possible that while in Worcester she had developed skills such as spinning and was able to use this expertise to earn a little money.

Marriage was the other option chosen by many young women in the hope of improving their lot. Walker says sometime after arriving in London Hannah made friends with a Dutch sailor, James Summs, and they married at the Fleet on 6 January 1744.[2] Hannah soon realised that she had made a

London from the Thames, 1746.

mistake in accepting Summs' hand in marriage and paid dearly for her poor judgement of character:

> But all his Promises of Friendship proved Instances of the highest Perfidy, and he turn'd out the worst and most unnatural of Husbands. Since, though she had Charms enough to captivate the Heart and secure the Affection of any reasonable Man, yet she was despised and condemned by her Husband, who not only kept criminal Company with other Women of the basest Characters, but also made away with her Things in Order to support his Luxury and the daily expenses of his Whores. (18)

Apparently while Summs was busy stealing and cheating, Hannah discovered that she was pregnant. As she grew larger, their marriage deteriorated even further and Summs fell into serious debt. Finally, when Hannah was seven months pregnant, her husband abandoned her, taking what was left of her possessions. Two months later she gave birth to a daughter and immediately moved back to Ship Street and into the care of her sister. As if the previous months had not been punishing enough for Hannah, her daughter became sickly and died seven months after her birth. Ever eager to remind his readers of Hannah's exemplary morals, Walker informs us that Hannah had her child "decently interred at her own expense" at St. George's Parish, Middlesex.

Clearly, Hannah's marriage had been a disaster. She had been treated cruelly by her husband, left destitute when most vulnerable, and forced to raise and then grieve for her daughter alone. Yet it is this tragic history that was to become the justification for her new identity:

> As she was now free from all the Ties arising from Nature and Consanguinity, she thought herself privileged to roam in quest of the Man who, without Reason, had injured her so much . . . That she might execute her Designs with the better Grace and the more Success, she boldly commenced a Man - at least in her Dress. (19)

Thus, according to Walker, Hannah made the decision to change her sex because she had little else to lose. In pursuit of her wayward husband, she assumed the identity of her brother-in-law, James Gray, and set off for Coventry on 23 November 1745. Like many accounts of female cross-dressers, Hannah's biography gives no description of the process she underwent to change her sex. Luckily, the 1740 biography of another female soldier, Christian Davies, gives us some idea of how Hannah may have made the transformation:

> Having thus ordered my affairs, I cut off my hair, and dressed me in a suit of my husband's, having had the precaution to quilt the waistcoat, to preserve my breasts from hurt, which were not large enough to betray my sex, and putting on the wig and hat I had prepared, I went out and bought me a silver-hilted sword, and some Holland shirts.[3]

While Hannah's change of sex is quite believable given the many documented examples of this phenomenon, Walker's justification is less than convincing. It is never established why Hannah was willing to risk her safety and travel from one end of England to the other in quest of a man described as the "worst and most unnatural of husbands".

There are a variety of reasons documented for women masquerading as men. The female pursuit of a male lover sent to war is probably the most common explanation cited in the many ballads sold on the streets at this time. However, patriotism, economic difficulty, fears for personal safety, a love of adventure, and the desire to live with another woman are also possible motivations. While there is no surviving evidence to suggest any other cause, Hannah's decision to change her sex as reported by Walker seems illogical, and a perverse twist to the literary convention of a woman's pursuit of her male lover.

3

Rebellion

W alker's description of Hannah's change of sex is notable for its lack of comment on the political upheaval occurring in England at that time. Only a fortnight before Hannah's supposed departure from London on 23 November 1745, Bonnie Prince Charlie and his Jacobite troops had crossed the Scottish border into England. On the very day Hannah set out for Coventry, it was reported in the *London Gazette* that the northern town of Carlisle had fallen to the rebels.[1] As Hannah moved north, the Jacobites were heading south towards her.

Understandably, there was a growing nervousness in London at the time and there can be no doubt that Hannah knew of the approaching threat. What woman in her right mind would dress as a man and head towards an invading army just as the government was conscripting able-bodied men to fight against it? The most obvious answer is that Hannah had been overwhelmed by a sense of patriotism, yet not once does Walker even hint that this might have been the driving force.

Walker's description of Hannah's first few months dressed as a man ranges from believable day-to-day detail to hyperbole. Four days after her departure from London, Hannah arrived in Coventry. Almost immediately she was pressed into Captain Miller's company, part of Colonel Guise's regiment, and she was billeted to a Mr Lucas in Little Park Street. Intent on concealing her true sex, she continued to make inquiries about her husband. Walker says that after three weeks in Coventry, Hannah and seventeen other new recruits were sent north to join Guise's regiment in Carlisle. The journey took the soldiers three weeks on foot and by the time they arrived at the town in early January 1746, the rebels had been chased back into Scotland by advancing British regiments.

Although Walker is unclear as to how long Hannah remained in Carlisle, his account of her stay is dominated by one event so improbable that it has provided ample ammunition to those who insist Hannah was a fraud. He says that Hannah was instructed in military exercises not long after her arrival in Carlisle and it was during this time that she became acquainted with a Sergeant Davis. The sergeant ordered Hannah to help him seduce a young woman. Hannah, struck by "a sudden emotion in her mind", visited the maid in question and warned her of the sergeant's intention. The woman was immensely grateful and, believing Hannah to be a young man, befriended her. When Davis subsequently approached his prospective victim, he realised that she had been warned off and suspected that Hannah, his accomplice, had now become his rival. Intent on revenge, he accused Hannah of neglect of duty and she was given 500 lashes while tied to the gates of Carlisle Castle.

Even Robert Walker appears to have had some trouble accounting for Hannah's ability (or desire) to conceal her sex under such arduous circumstances, and shrewdly notes that his justification comes from the mouth of the female soldier herself:

> Her Method was this, according to her own relation: At that Time her Breasts were but very small, and her Arms being extended and fix'd to the City Gates her breasts were towards the Wall, so that there was little or no Danger of her Comrades finding out the important Secret which she took such uncommon Pains to conceal. (141-142)

Assuming that Hannah had been able to survive the lashing, which is most unlikely, it is beyond all realms of credibility that while stripped to her waist and being beaten senseless, she could have concealed her sex.

Barely recovered from her injuries, the story continues with Hannah facing the greatest threat to her secret yet, when a new recruit, George Beck, joined Guise's regiment.[2] Walker claims that Beck was a young man from

Carlisle Castle, 1746.

Worcestershire who had recently been a lodger at the Grays' house in Wapping. Terrified that she would be recognised, Hannah deserted the army, swapped her regimental coat for one belonging to a pea picker and set out on a long but apparently uneventful journey from Carlisle to Portsmouth. However, in an effort to pad out his material, Walker returns to this journey later in his account and describes many amorous adventures Hannah had with other women on the way. While it is quite likely that Hannah did flirt with women, Walker sees these relationships as nothing more than an opportunity for a comical diversion.

It is questionable how much of Walker's account of Hannah's initial disguise and subsequent adventures in Carlisle we should believe. Comparing the description of events in contemporary records with Walker's narrative, we discover an account riddled with chronological time-shifts, where real events in Hannah's life have been reordered to change their emphasis.

The first time-shift in the biography relates to the birth and death of Hannah's daughter, Susannah. As we have seen, Walker claims Hannah married James Summs, who later abandoned her when she was pregnant. Her daughter then died seven months after her birth and, a short time later, on 27 November 1745, Hannah enlisted as a soldier in Coventry. However, the parish records for St. George-in-the-East, Middlesex, reveal that Susanna Sums, the daughter of James and Hanah Sums, was born *almost a year later* on or around 5 September 1746. The child was buried at six months of age, but on 31 January 1747. If we accept that Hannah joined the army in late 1745 but that her child was born a year later, her original motivation for transforming her sex - her husband's elopement and the death of her daughter - becomes redundant. What is even more extraordinary about the timing of the birth, according to Walker's chronology, is that Hannah must have become pregnant at the very time she claims to have been the victim of the flogging.

Baptisms - Day book, 1746, St. George-in-the-East, Middlesex.

While there is no doubt that either Hannah, Walker or both were distorting their account of Hannah's early military service, there are a number of details that are factually based. Captain Miller, whom Walker claims to have been Hannah's commanding officer, was a real historical figure. It has also been confirmed that the victualler to whom Hannah was supposedly billeted in Coventry, Mr Lucas, did indeed live in Little Park Street during this period.[3] However, it is quite likely that Walker picked up these details from somewhere other than Hannah.[4]

A further problem in believing Walker's account of Hannah's movements at this time is the fact that Guise's regiment was not even in England during the period of Hannah's supposed enlistment. The regiment passed through Coventry in mid-1744, but was in Scotland when Hannah journeyed to the town in late 1745.[5] Records also show that the regiment remained in Scotland during 1745 and 1746 and was not based in Carlisle until 1747, a year after Walker places Hannah there.[6]

The accumulation of evidence suggests that it is most unlikely that Hannah joined Guise's regiment in November 1745, unless we are prepared to accept that she joined the army, fell pregnant while dressed as a man, returned to London to have the child, was abandoned by James Summs and then subsequently resumed her male attire! Not only the first edition of Walker's biography, but also the publicity material of 1750 and official documents of the time tend to highlight Hannah's service in the marines rather than her years in the army, suggesting that she and her publicity machine did not wish to emphasise her unlikely involvement in the English resistance against the Jacobite invasion.

It seems likely that Hannah's adventures while dressed as a man between 1745 and late 1747 were pure fabrication. The tantalising question raised by this is that if later parts of the narrative are true, why bother fabricating these earlier adventures? In 1892, one observer proposed that it was Hannah's brother-in-law, James Gray, who served in Guise's regiment and later deserted. To save Gray from punishment, he says Gray's "sister-in-law's story not only protected him but proved a means of profit to herself".[7] While perhaps a conspiracy theory that stretches the bounds of probability, it is an interesting hypothesis, although it does not explain why Guise's regiment was incorrectly placed in Carlisle by Walker. It is evident that even as long ago as the 1890s, those pondering Hannah's story were feeling isolated from the events in her life and were frustrated by its contradictions.

4

A Passage to India

On 23 October 1747, the Royal Navy's sloop, the *Swallow*, lay anchored off the town of Portsmouth. The ship's captain, John Rowzier, noted in his log the arrival on board of "a lieutenant of marines and five private centinels".[1] Three of these men, Lieutenant Richard Wagget, John Hutchins and Dougal McDougal appear alongside Hannah's alias, James Gray, not only in Walker's biography but also naval and marine regimental records.[2] Walker says that Hannah was quartered on the *Swallow* with her fellow marines barely two months after her flight from Carlisle, and for the first time his narrative agrees closely with the historical records of the period.

At a time when the British and French were at war, the *Swallow* was part of a force commanded by Admiral Edward Boscawen, consisting of ten naval ships as well as vessels belonging to the East India Company. Aboard were 2000 soldiers, 800 of whom were marines, making it the largest European expedition that had ever sailed to the East Indies. As well as avenging the recent French capture of the English settlement of Madras, the object of the mission was to secure British supremacy in the region by seizing the strategic island of Mauritius and the Indian west coast town of Pondicherry - both then held by the French.

One cannot imagine what must have been going through Hannah's mind that afternoon as she was rowed out to her ship. Barely three times the length of a London bus, the *Swallow* squeezed 110 men into cramped conditions beneath its decks. How was it possible for a woman to conceal her sex in such a public living space for even a day, let alone two and a half years? Most accounts of female cross-dressers are coy about the physical practicalities a woman had to overcome to maintain her disguise, and Walker is no exception. It is difficult to comprehend how these women managed urination and menstruation while confined in this way. At the trial of one cross-dresser, Catherine Lincken, in 1721, it was revealed that she made use of "a leather-covered horn through which she urinated and [which she kept] fastened against her nude body".[3] One observer, Suzanne Stark, suggests that women could have used the toilets (located at the bow of the ship) when no one else was there. She also says that given the many physical problems on board, a female soldier's menstrual periods may have been perceived as just another ailment - perhaps venereal disease, which was then very common.[4] It is also possible that the extremely poor diet caused these women to stop menstruating altogether. While it seems an impossible feat, it must be remembered that sailors and soldiers on board washed very rarely and that as long as Hannah was vigilant, her shipmates may well have perceived her feminine body as that of an adolescent boy.

On 1 November 1747, the fleet weighed anchor and set out on its long journey to India. After battling heavy seas, the *Swallow* reached Lisbon on 2 December. During the trip to Portugal, Walker says Hannah's domestic talents had been noticed by her lieutenant, Richard Wagget, who

> asked her in a very friendly Manner to become one of their Mess . . . and from thence forward she acted in the Capacity of their Boy, and by her Knack in Cookery and her Care in washing their Linnen and mending their Shirts, &c. whenever they wanted repairing, she became a Favourite amongst them all, and was looked upon as the most handy Boy belonging to the Sloop. (31)

As would be expected, housekeeping was not Hannah's only activity while on the *Swallow*, and she was assigned a number of military duties:

> In Case of an Engagement, she was to be stationed upon the *Quarter-Deck,* and, as One of the *After-guard,* her Business was to fight and do what Mischief she could with the Small-Arms which they had on board, so that she was always in readiness in Case of an Attack. (31)

On Christmas eve, after three weeks of repairs in Lisbon, the *Swallow* set sail for Cape Town accompanied by the *Vigilant*. Within hours of their departure the two ships were separated by large seas and the *Swallow* struggled to stay afloat: "In short, she lost the best Part of her new Rigging, and was damaged to that Degree, even in her Hold, that all Hands were obliged to be busy, and the Pump was for ever going" (35). Captain Rowzier knew that the sloop was in danger and rather than attempt to return to Lisbon, took advantage of a strong easterly and headed for Gibraltar.[5] By the time the ship reached the British colony, Richard Wagget had fallen seriously ill and was taken onto the island for immediate care. Walker says that Hannah accompanied her lieutenant and nursed him out of danger.

The *Swallow* left Gibraltar on 29 January 1748 and headed south towards Cape Town. Again it was a hard journey, intermittently relieved by the

Gibraltar

taking on of supplies at Madeira and the Cape Verde islands.[6] After what must have seemed a particularly unlucky journey, the *Swallow* joined the rest of the fleet at Cape Town on 6 May. Admiral Boscawen was pleased by their safe arrival, believing them lost, and reported to the Admiralty: "Yesterday arrived here His Majesty's sloop the *Swallow*, all well on board, not having buried but one man since they left England, and in other respects in a better condition than any ship of the squadron".[7]

Only two days after Hannah and her mates had arrived in Cape Town, Boscawen ordered the fleet to weigh anchor and head for Mauritius. They arrived on 23 June. The following day, Boscawen ordered the sloop to undertake a survey of the island's coast. He received the *Swallow's* report on 25 June and it was decided that a small landing party should kidnap a French soldier from the shore in order to ascertain the enemy's strength. The next morning Boscawen was informed that the attempt had been foiled by a large reef running along the coast which prevented the landing party getting on shore. While the Admiral deliberated upon this news, Hannah, her fellow marines, and thirty volunteer seamen aboard the *Swallow* were preparing themselves to attack the island. Boscawen called a Council of War and it was decided that, while there was no doubt that their force was large enough to take the island, it was probable that they would be left with insufficient numbers to undertake the invasion of Pondicherry - a task which they considered the primary objective of their mission.[8]

The attack was called off and, luckily for Hannah, her first experience of war was postponed. The fleet left Mauritius on 28 June and headed directly for the Coromandel Coast of India, where, at Pondicherry, the French were busily preparing themselves for the arrival of the powerful British force.

5

The Siege of Pondicherry

Hannah and her mates sailed into the English settlement of Fort St. David (twelve miles south of Pondicherry) on 27 July. They would not have known that their commanding officers were working to a tight deadline because of the approaching monsoon season, or that some officials in India were worried that the French were too well prepared for the English attack. At around the time of the *Swallow's* arrival, the Naval Commander-in-Chief of the East Indies, Admiral Thomas Griffin, expressed his doubts to the Admiralty about the viability of the expedition:

> Mr Boscawen is gone Against Pondicherry, which I fear he will not find so easy a Conquest as many People have imagined, for they have been throwing up Works ever since the beginning of December . . . However I hope they will take it, but think more men would be necessary to Execute the rest of the Plan.[1]

Since leaving Gibraltar, those travelling on the *Swallow* had spent only twelve days on land out of the previous six months and the thought of disembarking to commence a siege must have seemed a mixed blessing. Before light, on the morning of 31 July, the *Swallow's* marines were sent ashore and ordered to set up camp two miles out of Fort St. David. Preparations for the battle continued until both the marine and East India Company battalions, as well as three thousand Indian troops and porters, were ready to commence marching.

Robert Walker gives away nothing of Hannah's personal feelings as she set off for battle. He talks only of her bravery and fighting skills, and perhaps Hannah herself, when recounting her story to Walker, chose not to reveal any fears she may have had. Just the experience of being in India for the first time, let alone the trials of war, must have been overwhelming for Hannah - the white beaches edged with palm trees, the humid heat, the black-skinned locals, and unfamiliar foods. Did it ever occur to her while on her travels that her disguise may have been less effective in a region dominated by different cultures and dress codes?[2] If the locals did happen to notice Hannah's deception, it seems nothing was said to her fellow marines or officers.

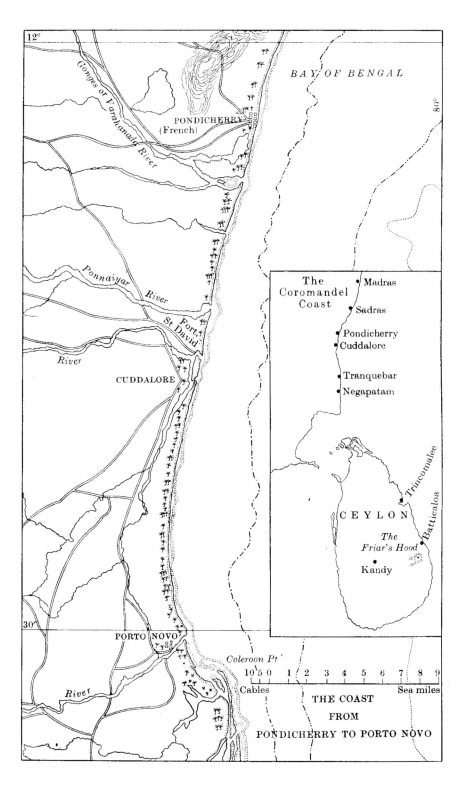

12°

Gonges or Varahanadi River

BAY OF BENGAL

80°

PONDICHERRY
(French)

Ponnaiyar River

Fort
St David

River

CUDDALORE

PORTO NOVO

30'

Coleroon Pt

River

The Coromandel Coast

- Madras
- Sadras
- Pondicherry
- Cuddalore
- Tranquebar
- Negapatam

CEYLON

The Friar's Hood

- Kandy

Trincomalee

Batticaloa

10 5 0   1   2   3   4   5   6   7   8   9

Cables   Sea miles

THE COAST
FROM
PONDICHERRY TO PORTO NOVO

On 8 August, taking advantage of the cool of the early morning, the English battalions marched towards the French fort of Ariancoupan (situated only four miles from Pondicherry), each soldier carrying his own tent poles, hatchet, camp kettle and musket.[3] They encamped near the fort on 10 August, but it was to be nine days before the French abandoned their position. The English took possession of Ariancoupan, then in order to boost the number of troops at his disposal, Boscawen had 1100 sailors trained in manual exercises and sent ashore to join the existing army. On 26 August, the British marched closer towards Pondicherry and began to dig trenches and set up their cannons.

In what was an almost unprecedented move, the Admiralty had made Boscawen Commander-in-Chief of both land and sea operations, and a number of commentators have since questioned the wisdom of this dual responsibility.[4] Boscawen has been criticised for approaching Pondicherry from the south-west, forcing his troops not only to waste precious days laying siege against the relatively insignificant fort of Ariancoupan, but also to ford the Ariancoupan River before reaching the citadel.

For a month, Hannah and her fellow soldiers lay in their trenches, inching closer towards the thick walls of Pondicherry. The English were subjected to a continual barrage of gunfire and mortars, with little sign of achieving their objective. To make matters worse, the weather had begun to turn and, as early as 10 September, one of Hannah's fellow soldiers, James Miller, wrote about the unbearable conditions:

> We have had very bad weather of late, the Rains have been so great that our Trenches is fill'd with water and Mud, being almost unpassable, being so deep that it takes us to the wast [sic] and are oblg'd [sic] to stand in them twenty four hours and to pass and repass everything to the assistance of our Brother Soldiers. The Duty is very hard upon us, having scarce a night's rest in a week.[5]

The expedition had run out of time and the monsoon was beginning to set in. Despite the hopelessness of the situation, the English continued to fight on for another three weeks until it was clear to all that the siege would have to be raised:

> It was therefore thought impossible to reduce the Town this Season, the Monsoons beginning to set and the Rains to fall very heavy, which greatly harass'd our Men, we being so weaken'd by Deaths and Sickness that some were obliged to be on Duty two or three Days together, and those that

mounted the Trenches were obliged to sit all that Time up to their Breech in Water. (Walker, 53-54)

It seems extraordinary that Hannah claimed not only to have endured these horrendous conditions, but that she also managed to maintain her disguise throughout this period. It is during the last week of the collapsing siege that Walker's account and the naval records seriously disagree as to the state of Hannah's health when she left the battlefield. Walker claims that the female marine was seriously injured in the dying days of the campaign:

> She stood so deep in Water, she fired no less than thirty-seven Rounds of Shot, and during the Engagement received six Shot in her Right Leg and five in the Left, and what affected her more than all the Rest, one so dangerous in the Groin . . . she remained all that Day and the following Night in the Camp before she was carried to the Hospital, and after that she was brought there and laid in Kit she continued till next Day in the greatest Agony and Pain. (58)

Yet despite this graphic account of Hannah's suffering, official ships' musters tell quite another story. On 30 September, Boscawen ordered his troops to retreat and return to their ships. Hannah's alter ego, James Gray, and a number of his fellow marines were transferred from the *Swallow* to the *Eltham*, man-of-war.[6] All the records documenting the transfer, as well as the musters for the entire battle, show that James Gray was fit and well and had not once been absent due to injury. While Walker would rather have us believe that Gray spent three months lying in hospital after Pondicherry, the *Eltham's* musters reveal that at the very same time, he was actually busy sailing from Fort St. David to Bombay without the slightest hint of ill-health.

6

The Mystery of Hannah's Wounds

Walker's description of Hannah being shot down in the trenches of Pondicherry contributed greatly to her popularity in 1750. The intense publicity concentrated on this one event more than any other in her notable life. Given the importance of this incident to the selling of the story, it seems extraordinary that naval records do not show that James Gray was either injured or struck down by illness at Pondicherry. However, before we are tempted to dismiss the Snell story completely, we must remember that in Walker's description of Hannah's earlier life discrepancies between the biography and official records were more often the result of time-shifts than outright fabrication.

The following is Walker's rather patchy description of Hannah's adventures after the siege of Pondicherry, between late September 1748 and October 1749. Sometime in September, he says, Hannah was severely wounded and transported to the main hospital at Cuddelore, just south of Fort St. David. Her secret now faced its greatest test and despite the extent of her injuries, Hannah resisted informing her doctor, Mr Belchier, about the bullet in her groin. She then removed the bullet herself and treated the wound with ointments she had purchased from an Indian nurse working in the hospital.

It supposedly took three months for Hannah to convalesce, during which time her ship, the *Eltham,* had sailed to Madras with the rest of the fleet. When Hannah was eventually discharged from the hospital, the *Eltham* had not yet returned and she was sent aboard the *Tartar* where she performed the duties of a common sailor. Walker appears intentionally hazy about when these events actually happened, his vague chronology implying that Hannah left Cuddelore hospital in early January 1749.[1]

Not long after Hannah had joined the *Tartar,* Walker says the *Eltham* returned from Madras and she was sent aboard. They then set sail for Bombay and despite the ship being very old and leaky somehow managed to sail from the west coast to the east coast of India in less than a fortnight. The *Eltham* and its crew was stationed at Bombay for five weeks while the ship underwent extensive repairs. During this time at port, Walker says

Hannah was involved in a serious conflict with the First Lieutenant of the ship, George Allen. He claims Allen ordered Hannah to sing a song for him, but she refused. Allen then accused Hannah of stealing a shirt, had her clapped in irons for five days, ordered that she receive twelve lashes and that she "continued at the foretop for four hours". Once again, Hannah is the victim of a senior officer's malice in an incident reminiscent of the Sergeant Davis affair in Carlisle.

According to Walker, the *Eltham* then returned to Fort St. David, which was soon struck by a massive hurricane, sinking many of the expedition's ships, including the flagship, the *Namur*, on which six hundred men were lost. Records reveal that this great loss to the navy occurred on 13 April 1749, and Walker tells us nothing more of Hannah's life between this date and her departure from India six months later.[2]

Let us now compare Walker's version of events with surviving naval documents (see table). The *Eltham* musters not only reveal that James Gray survived the siege of Pondicherry unscathed in late 1748, but also give us an idea of how Gray occupied his time during the following year. On 24 October 1748, the *Eltham* set sail for Bombay with Gray on board. The ship was leaking badly, and during the journey almost half the crew became ill with scurvy. Curiously, Walker chose not to mention this fact, which would have spiced his story nicely. The ship arrived in Bombay on 3 January, over nine weeks after its departure (not two weeks, as in the biography). It was repaired and cleaned in Bombay and remained in the area for the next four months. Given that the *Eltham* did not leave Bombay until 3 May, it is impossible for the ship to have been a victim of the April hurricane that hit Fort St. David. Those aboard the *Eltham* were, in fact, shocked to discover the wreck of the *Namur* on their return to the settlement in late May.

While Walker's description of Hannah's life in India virtually ends in April 1749, the *Eltham's* musters reveal that James Gray was involved in a second siege between June and August of that year. Influenced by his involvement in Indian politics, Boscawen ordered a force of eleven ships to sail to Porto Novo and to seize the Fort of Devicotta. On 29 May the *Eltham* anchored off Porto Novo, with James Gray, his fellow marines, and a battalion of East India Company soldiers aboard. On 11 June, the marines were sent ashore and the following day the fort was seized. Unfortunately there is no information on Gray's level of involvement in the operations, but we know the marines came back on board the *Eltham* on 13 June.[3] The

Eltham stayed at Porto Novo for a further six weeks, returning to Fort St. David on 1 August.

The *Eltham's* musters of the following day reveal startling information which partly vindicates Walker's claims about Hannah's hospitalisation. On 2 August, a month and a half after the attack on Devicotta, James Gray was indeed admitted to Cuddelore Hospital and remained there for over two months under the care of William Belchier.[4] While Gray was in hospital, the *Eltham* did sail to Madras and on his release, he was sent to the *Tartar,* boarding on 7 October.[5] A week later he returned on board the *Eltham* and the fleet set sail for England on 19 October. Once more Walker has clearly used his time-shift technique to suit his own narrative purposes. The expedition's activities at Pondicherry were well reported back in England and would have been familiar to the biography's readers - no doubt a good incentive for Walker to place Hannah in hospital as a result of Pondicherry rather than the little-known skirmish at Devicotta.

Event	Facts	Walker
Leaves Fort St. David	24 Oct 1748	ca Jan 1749
Arrives Bombay	3 Jan 1749	ca Jan 1749
Storm at Fort St. David	13 Apr 1749	ca Apr 1749
Leaves Bombay	3 May 1749	ca Mar 1749
Arrives Fort St. David	19 May 1749	ca Mar 1749
Sails to Porto Novo	29 May 1749	no mention
Siege of Devicotta	12 Jun 1749	no mention
Sails to Fort St. David	1 Aug 1749	no mention
Sent to Cuddelore Hospital	2 Aug 1749	ca Sep 1748
Joins Tartar	7 Oct 1749	ca Jan 1749
Joins Eltham	15 Oct 1749	ca Jan 1749
Leaves for England	19 Oct 1749	19 Nov 1749
Wagget dies	21 Oct 1749	20 Nov 1749

This table compares the biography's chronology with that of the naval musters and clearly illustrates Walker's time-shifts.

N°	Time of			Whence and whether Preſt or not.	N° and Letter of Tickets.	Mens Names.
	Entry.	Year.	Appearance.			
1	Oct. 9	1748	Oct. 9th	Swallow		Rd. Waggett
						Geo. Hunley
						Jas. Chadd
						Robt. Richardson
5						Jno. Hutchings
						Jas. Hays
ſo Sent S. Geo. Hospt. 2. Sep. 1749 retd. 4o. 7th. Oct. Do.						Wm. Green
						Hen: Hall
						Edwd. Jeffreys
ſo Cuddelore Hospl. 2. Aug. 1749 retd. from the Tartar 13. Oct. Do.						Jas. Gray
						Jno. Hanley

This Extract from the Eltham musters details James Gray's admittance into Cuddelore Hospital on 2 August 1749. It also shows Gray's transferral from the Tartar back to the Etham.

There are many questions surrounding the hospitalisation of James Gray. What was wrong with Gray - had he been injured at Devicotta, or struck down by disease? Unfortunately, neither the records of the *Eltham's* surgeon nor of Cuddelore Hospital have survived, and one is left guessing as to the cause of illness.

Did Hannah receive eleven wounds in her legs and one in her groin at Devicotta rather than at Pondicherry? Could she have survived wounds as serious as these for six weeks on the *Eltham* before reaching hospital? Would her sex not have been discovered under such extreme conditions? Does it seem possible that having arrived at Cuddelore, Hannah would have been able to continue hiding her sex, despite her wounds, for a further two months?

While hygiene conditions were poor and there are examples of other female soldiers concealing their wounds in hospital, a disease such as scurvy or malaria seems a more plausible diagnosis than battle injuries, which would have required a more thorough examination.[6] Supporting the hypothesis that Hannah was ill with disease rather than battle injuries are the number of *Eltham* crew falling ill and dying at this time. Twenty members of the crew were sent to either Cuddelore or Fort St. George hospitals in August and September, and a further six marines died without ever entering hospital.[7] Importantly, almost as many sailors as marines were being treated, and as it is unlikely that these sailors were involved in the siege at Devicotta, we must look elsewhere for the cause of their illness.

While we may never know whether the marines and sailors were being treated for the same ailment, there is no doubt that an increased level of illness was affecting the *Eltham's* crew. Walker's account of Hannah's hospitalisation appears to be based on fact, and given the higher incidence of illness aboard the *Eltham* it is possible that Hannah contracted a disease and managed to maintain her disguise throughout the period she spent under care. Such a hypothesis explains why Walker and Hannah found it necessary to manufacture Hannah's wounds at Pondicherry, as without them, she was not entitled to a military pension.

7

Homeward Bound

On Thursday 19 October 1749, the *Eltham* started its long journey back to England.[1] Hannah, barely a fortnight out of hospital, was probably still weak and tired. Any feeling of unease she may have had about her future was exacerbated by the death of her friend and master, Lieutenant Richard Wagget, who had died only a day after their departure from Fort St. David:[2]

> This Loss shock'd our Heroine greatly, for he was the only sincere Friend she had on board, and the only one in Case of any Insult she could have recourse to for any Redress. . . . She was taken Notice of, soon after the Death of her dear Friend Mr Wygate [Wagget], by Mr Kite, who was second Lieutenant of the Ship, and admitted into his immediate Service, in which she continued for about two Months . . . having got a Boy to attend him, he recommended her to Mr Wallace [Wallis], the third Lieutenant of the Ship, who . . . proved very kind and indulgent to her during the whole Voyage.
>
> (69-71)

Hannah's five months in the service of Samuel Wallis marks a curious moment in history, as both individuals were to be later celebrated in entirely different fields. Wallis (1728-1795) was only twenty-two years old when he took on James Gray as his servant, but seventeen years later he was known as the first European to discover Tahiti.

The *Eltham* arrived at Cape Town in late December, remaining there a month while repairs were made to the ship and supplies loaded for the journey to Lisbon. Not long after their departure, on 24 January, Walker mentions that Hannah became the focus of her shipmates' jibes and earned the nickname "Miss Molly Gray"[3] because of her inability to grow a beard:

> As these Taunts, however, were only thrown out in Jest, she would return the Compliment not only with a Smile and an Oath but with a Challenge of the best Sailor of them all . . . Tho' she seemed not to resent the unlucky Nickname they had given her, for very prudential Reasons, yet it secretly created her many an uneasy Hour. (71-72)

During the return journey Walker alternates between episodes that exaggerate Hannah's false masculinity with moments that remind us of her vulnerability. Not long after their arrival in Lisbon on 11 April 1750, Hannah vowed to throw off the nickname of "Miss Molly Gray" once and for all. She accompanied the ship's crew into town where "she play'd the Part of a boon Companion so naturally, and so far distant from what bore the least Appearance to Effeminacy, that she answer'd the End proposed. The Name of *Miss Molly* was here perfectly buried in Oblivion" (73). As in many episodes of the narrative, Hannah is required to feign "impurity" to protect her "purity", and Walker says that while in Lisbon, Hannah and a mate, Edward Jefferies, drew lots for a prostitute who had attached herself to Hannah (inevitably Hannah drew the short straw and, once more, her secret remained secure).

Walker describes a moment of deep introspection following a conversation in a Lisbon tavern, when Hannah learns of the fate of her absent husband. A sailor formerly acquainted with Summs informs Hannah that after leaving his wife, the deserter worked on various ships, sailing to Amsterdam and Cork, before finally landing in Genoa. Within weeks of his arrival in Italy he fell into an argument with a local gentleman and fatally stabbed him. Summs was sentenced to death - he was placed in a hessian bag filled with stones and thrown into the harbour.[4] While there is no evidence for or against this anecdote, it acts as a literary device freeing Hannah from her official quest, the death of her husband allowing her to resume her former life.

Lisbon Harbour

On 7 May 1750, the *Eltham* weighed anchor at Lisbon and set out for Portsmouth on what was to be this leaky man-of-war's final journey in the service of His Majesty's Navy.[5] The ship arrived on Friday 25 May and Hannah "went on Shore the very Day of her Arrival and took Lodgings, together with several of her Comrades and Fellow-travellers at the Sign of the 'Jolly Marine and Sailor' in Portsmouth" (101).[6] The marines spent a drunken weekend celebrating their freedom, and Walker regales us with tales of Hannah wooing a young woman and

> by this Stratagem she got rid of her raking, drunken Companions without giving the least Disgust, and spent her Hours less extravagantly, and at the same Time more agreeably in the familiar Conversation with Mrs Catherine.
> (104)

On Monday 27 May, Hannah set out for London in the company of ten marines belonging to her regiment. Walker says that to help defray costs, each man was paid five shillings "conduct money" prior to their departure, a detail which is recorded in the Marines' regimental accounts.[7] It took three days for the soldiers to reach London via Petersfield and Guildford. It was probably on the evening of 30 May that Hannah knocked at the door of her sister's house and

> notwithstanding our Heroine's Appearance in Masquerade, her Sister knew her almost at the first Glance, and ventured, contrary to all seeming Decency and good Manners, to throw her Arms about our young Marine's Neck, and almost stifled her with Kisses. (119)

At last, Robert Walker had brought his heroine safely home.

8

Fame

W alker tells us that on Saturday 9 June 1750, Hannah set in motion the process of publicly dismantling her masquerade, little knowing where it would lead her. While she had already informed her sister and brother-in-law, it was time to break the news to her old shipmates. That morning she and a number of her fellow marines made their way to Downing Street and the house of John Winter, agent to their regiment. There must have been an air of excitement among the soldiers, given that many were about to receive payment for years of service. Hannah had two-and-a-half years' pay due to her and Walker says she received fifteen pounds along with two suits, which she sold almost immediately for sixteen shillings.[1]

To celebrate their new wealth, the group went to a nearby tavern. From Walker's account it appears that Susannah and James were waiting there for Hannah - to give moral support as she prepared to make her announcement to her fellow marines:

> The Money now being paid, and our Heroine having been determined to raise all the ready Cash she could before she opened a new Scene, which she well knew would amuse them - I mean, an open and ingenious Discovery of a Secret that had been so long kept close, and which she purposed to reveal before they parted, prudently considering that she should never perhaps have so favourable an Opportunity again of disclosing her Sex to such a Number of Witnesses at once, who would at any Time afterwards be ready to testify the Truth of all her merry Adventures.   (155-156)

If Walker's description is accurate, it seems that her decision to profit from her unique situation had been made with a sense of urgency, before the story had grown cold and the witnesses had dispersed. Hannah was no doubt counting on her friends to confirm her identity but expected them not to be overly concerned with her embroidery of the tale she later told the public.

Walker says that Hannah's friends were shocked by her revelation, at first believing it to be "one of Jemmy's merry conceits to amuse them", but were ultimately convinced when Susannah and James "assured them that they would attest the Truth of this Metamorphosis, if the Company required it, upon Oath" (158). Once they had recovered from this news, a number of

Hannah's friends suggested that she should submit a petition to the Captain-General of the British Army, the Duke of Cumberland, in which she should ask for financial recompense for the injuries she had received while serving in the marines.

Taking up this advice, on 16 June Hannah approached the Duke's carriage while it was stationary at St. James' Park. Dressed in a man's suit, she handed the Duke her petition, who immediately read it and then ordered his Adjutant-General, Colonel Napier, to test the authenticity of her claims.[2] A week later, on 23 June, *The Whitehall Evening Post* broke the whole story when it reported Hannah's meeting with Cumberland:

> Last week one Hannah Snell, born at Worcester, who was seven Years in a Marine Regiment by the Name of James Gray, went to the East Indies in Admiral Boscawen's Squadron, and was at the siege of Pondicherry, presented a Petition to his Royal Highness the Duke of Cumberland, praying some provision might be made for her now she is discharged the Service. His Royal Highness referred her petition to general Fraser; to report it to him, and make her a suitable Provision according to her Merit. It seems her sweetheart being impressed into the Marine Service, she put on Men's Cloaths, and entered in the same Regiment, went to the East-Indies in the same Ship with him, and was his messmate while he lived (he dying in the Voyage) and was as Servant to one of the lieutenants. She behaved with great Intrepidity as a Sailor and Soldier, and her Sex was never discovered by either her Sweetheart or any of her Comrades till she made the Discovery herself by the above-mentioned Petition.[3]

This account of Hannah's life is barely recognisable - a romanticised conglomerate of female soldier ballads, gossip and half-reported facts. Interestingly, this confused description of Hannah's adventures appears almost to suggest a relationship between Hannah and Wagget (although it would be foolhardy to view such an unreliable source as anything more than an indication of the cultural baggage carried by Hannah's story).

Given the confused accounts appearing in the newspapers at this time, we can only be grateful that Walker's biography is as factually based as it is. Yet the facts surrounding his own relationship with Hannah are almost as hazy as the early press reports. Robert Walker was a maverick figure in the publishing world of this period. He was a prolific producer of both pirated and original editions covering a wide variety of subjects, and is regarded as an innovator in the serialisation of books as well as a leading figure in the fledgling provincial press.[4] Walker was an adventurous businessman who was not averse to sensationalism and it is no surprise that he would try and monopolise the rights to Hannah's adventures.

It is not known when Walker discovered Hannah's story or which of the two parties first approached the other, but the two names were first linked on 27 June in an affidavit presented by Hannah to the Lord Mayor of London, John Blachford.[5] The document served two purposes: firstly, it summarised Hannah's adventures in male dress, carefully emphasising her injuries and, secondly, ensured Robert Walker's sole possession of the Snell story:

> [Snell] lastly saith, That she has not given the least Hint of her surprising Adventures to any other Person, nor will she . . . give the least Account thereof, to any Person whatsoever, to be printed or published, save and except the above-mentioned Robert Walker.

At the bottom of the document lies the signature of Hannah, her sister and, most importantly for publicity reasons, the Lord Mayor. There is no doubt that the affidavit was prepared by Hannah's publisher, as it contains his telltale time-shifts. Significantly, the document notes that Hannah was present at "the Siege of Pondicherry, and all other sieges during that expedition". While perhaps a slip of the pen, this is the only time Walker intimates that Hannah was at the siege of Devicotta.

The next day, a copy of the affidavit was splashed across the London newspapers, advertising the forthcoming release of the biography.[6] This small, 46 page leatherbound edition, priced at one shilling, appeared on the streets on 3 July. Despite its brevity, this biography was eventually to determine history's impression of its subject. Walker confirms that this edition was quickly thrown together, possibly within a week or two:

> As this Treatise was done in a Hurry from Hannah Snell's own mouth, and directly committed to the Press, occasioned by the impatience of the Town to have it published, it is not doubted but that such Part of it as appears incorrect will be candidly overlook'd, that, being made up in the veracity and fullness of her surprising Adventures; the like not to be met with in the Records of Time. (1st edition, 43)

Despite this disclaimer, Walker made few amendments to the basic structure of the story when he released the first of a nine-part serialised edition on 14 July.[7] Instead, he chose simply to expand and elaborate upon the many anecdotes of the first edition - apparently confident that the public had accepted his interpretation of the story hook, line and sinker.

While the hurried release of the second edition is indicative of the level of public interest in Hannah at the time, it is only one aspect of a major publicity campaign. To what degree the campaign was orchestrated rather than accidental is difficult to say. Walker was probably responsible for the widespread promotion of the book in many newspapers and magazines across England,[8] but there were also at least four separate portraits of Hannah being sold on the streets by mid-July.[9]

The most immediate feature of this publicity campaign, however, was Hannah's appearances on the London stage. On 29 June, the *General Advertiser* carried a small advertisement announcing that Hannah would be performing a "New Song" that evening at the New Wells theatre, in Goodman's Fields. Under the management of William Hallam, the New Wells specialised almost exclusively in harlequinades, with such offerings as rope-dancing, acrobatics, and dramatic recreations of popular historical events. With performances commencing at five o'clock and running as long as five hours, Hannah was only one act among many.

The Whitehall and General Evening Post captured the atmosphere of

"The English Heroine or the British Amazon." A portrait of Hannah sold in 1750.

Hannah's opening night:

> Last Night there were the greatest Number of reputable Persons ever known
> at the New Wells, Goodman's Fields, to see and hear the famous Hannah
> Snell sing two songs. She appeared in her Marine Habit, and met with
> universal Applause, as she behaved with great Decency and good manners.[10]

One suspects that this commentator may have been a little disappointed
by Hannah's "decency and good manners", perhaps hoping for something a
little wilder.[11] A combination of newspaper advertisements and Walker's
description gives us a clear picture of what the audience at the New Wells
experienced that night, as well as later in the season when the act became
more complicated.

Between 29 June and 6 September, Hannah made sixty appearances in
only seventy days, performing every night except Sundays.[12] In the first
three weeks of the season, her performances were limited to one or two
songs, and Walker is candid about her vocal ability:

> Now in the Performance of this Branch of her province it must be allowed
> that Art and the Airs of a Player are less conspicuous in her than in those
> who have long made Singing on the Stage their principal Profession. But
> then Nature steps in and amply supplies that Deficiency. She puts on no
> affected, no studied Airs to embellish the Words of her Poet; neither has she,
> in reality, as she will readily enough and modestly acknowledge, any
> acquired Judgement in Musick, to add new Graces to the several Catches
> which she exhibits; but then her Action is free, easy, and without Affectation,
> and Nature has given her such a Voice that renders her Service in that Way
> highly acceptable to the Publick, and that too in such a Manner that she is
> obliged to repeat her Operations to gratify the Audience. (174)

Hannah's performance was obviously pleasing enough, because on 19 July
the *General Advertiser* announced that in addition to her "New Songs" she
would "go thro' all the manual exercises of a soldier in her regimentals".
Walker is more generous about her military displays than her vocal ones:

> In this Branch of her Office she appears regularly dress'd in her Regimentals
> from Top to Toe, with all the Accoutrements requisite for the due
> Performance of her Military Exercises.
>   Here she and her Attendants fill up the Stage in a very agreeable Manner.
> The Tabor and Drum give a Life to her March, and she traverses the Stage
> two or three Times over, Step by Step, in the same Manner as our soldiers
> march on the Parade in St. James's Park.

Hannah Snell *in Her* Regimentals *as she performs the Manual Exercise of a* Soldier *at Goodmans Fields Wells* 1750.

Join ỹ right Hand to ỹ Firelock.

Present and Fire

Charge ỹ Bayonet Breast High.

Rest your Bayonet on ỹ left Arm

Hannah performing her Manual Exercises in 1750.

After the Spectators have been sufficiently amused with this formal Procession, she begins her Military Exercises, and goes thro' the whole Catechism (If I may be allowed the Expression) with so much Dexterity and Address, and with so little Hesitation or Default, that great Numbers even of Veteran Soldiers, who have resorted to the Wells out of mere Curiosity only, have frankly acknowledged that she executes what she undertakes to Admiration.   (175-176)

Hannah continued performing this act for a further six weeks, adding additional songs to her repertoire in the last days of August.[13] It was a long season for someone with no experience on the stage, but was no doubt lucrative. The exact details of the financial arrangement between Hannah and William Hallam are unknown, but Walker says that Hannah

induced the Manager of the said House to enter into a Contract with her to pay her weekly Salary for the Season, which is such a Stipend that not one Woman in ten thousand of her low Extraction and want of Literature could, by any Act of Industry (how laborious soever) with any Possibility procure.
(165-166)

Hannah's promoters knew that the public would eventually tire of her and encouraged her to exploit her popularity while she could:

As it is not natural to suppose that the Martial Exercises of our Heroine can continue long to be an Entertainment to the Town, or that her Singing in the Manner that she does, which is agreeable enough whilst it is received as a Novelty, can stand the Test any longer than the present Season, our Heroine and Actress is determined to make Hay whilst the Sun shines, and, like the laborious Ant, to lay up a little Stock to support her against a rainy Day.
(177-178)

After a run of sixty consecutive advertisements in the *General Advertiser,* Hannah's season at Goodman's Fields came to an end on 6 September. She chose not, however, to abandon her stage career entirely. An advertisement appeared in the *General Advertiser* on 11 September, announcing, "for one night only", Hannah's appearance at the New Wells Spa, Clerkenwell.[14] The season was extended for a further four nights but - whether limited by Hannah's exhaustion or the public's lack of interest - it then closed. Whatever the reason, one could say that Hannah's stage career went out with a whimper rather than a bang. For the second time in less than four months, she was not only forced to contemplate her future, but perhaps even the sex by which she would pursue the next stage of her life.

9

A Question of Money

An important part of Hannah's grand plan for her financial security was to obtain a pension from the authorities. In fact, Hannah was hoping to receive two pensions, one from the Duke of Cumberland and the other from the Royal Chelsea Hospital (the institution responsible for those injured while serving in the Army or Marines).[1]

While we know that the Royal Hospital obliged, it appears that the Duke was not so forthcoming, despite some accounts to the contrary. On 27 June, a little over a week after Hannah had presented her petition to Cumberland, and just prior to her debut on stage, the *Penny London Post* made note of

> a report having been made to the Duke of Cumberland, by his order, of the truth of the petition of Hannah Snell . . . his Royal Highness has been pleased to order her to be put upon the King's List, by which she will obtain a pension of thirty pounds per annum, for her life.[2]

There is no evidence that Hannah ever received this pension and, as late as mid-August, Walker tartly comments upon the Duke's lack of action:

> What his Royal Highness however may possibly do for her hereafter rests still undetermined, and we must content ourselves (since he has not thought fit to exert his Bounty and Benevolence towards her as yet) with wishing (as we have done before) that it may be some farther annual Pension, in order to enable her to spend the Remainder of her Days in some Degree of Credit and Reputation. (177)

It is intriguing to ponder why the Duke was reluctant to grant Hannah a pension. One possible explanation is that he was not particularly interested in this odd specimen of a soldier, as there is no record of Hannah being mentioned in any of his surviving papers, which are extensive.[3] Alternatively, Cumberland may simply not have believed her story, despite Colonel Napier having delivered a certificate verifying Hannah's wounding at Pondicherry.[4]

Whatever the reason, it appears not to have influenced those on the Royal Hospital Board. On 21 November 1750, "Hannah Snell, alias James Gray", was admitted as an out pensioner to the Royal Hospital.[5] The

Hospital's admission roll records the event:

2nd Mars. [Marines] ffrazer's [Frazier's regiment], Hannah Snell, age 27. Time of service $4^1/_2$ years in this & Guise's Regt. Wounded at Pondicherry in the thigh and both leggs, born at Worcester, her father a Dyer.[6]

The Board's acceptance of Hannah as an out pensioner raises some very curious questions. Is it only a coincidence that the entry in the admission roll reads like an extract from Walker's biography? If government records 250 years old show us that James Gray was not wounded at Pondicherry, surely officials at the Hospital in 1750 must have been equally aware of the situation. Was the granting of Hannah's pension the result of bureaucratic incompetence or collusion? There is no record of the commissioners of the Hospital discussing Hannah's case during their board meetings in 1750, so we can only speculate as to what lay behind their ultimate decision.[7]

Hannah was only one of two women knowingly granted a pension by the Royal Hospital. The other, Christian Davies, or Mother Ross, was reported to have received a pension after many years of service at the beginning of the eighteenth century. Unconfirmed sources say Davies was buried at Chelsea Hospital with military honours in 1739.[8] Yet once again, we do not have records revealing the machinations behind the decision to grant this financial recognition.

Let us assume for a moment that Hannah applied for her pension like any other soldier. Firstly, her regimental agent, John Winter, would have appeared at Chelsea Hospital attesting to the authenticity of certificates

Chelsea Hospital, 1748.

documenting her wounds. Then, on 21 November, she would have presented herself to the Hospital doctor for a physical examination. However, given Hannah's sex, and the fact that the Duke of Cumberland had been involved in the case, it is quite possible that Hannah was not required to apply for her pension like other soldiers. Considering that Colonel Napier, one of the army's most senior officers, had already prepared certificates that authenticated Hannah's wounds, the Royal Hospital probably felt it had all the evidence it needed. Perhaps Hannah was not even required to undertake a physical examination or, if she did, scars possibly collected at Devicotta were attributed to Pondicherry.

If the Royal Hospital had relied on Napier's report, how could his office have got things so wrong? We will probably never know. Perhaps only a cursory glance was made at ship and hospital musters to confirm James Gray's participation in the Boscawen expedition, or else, for some unknown reason, the military was willing to accommodate Hannah's lie.[9] The motivation for such collusion is difficult to justify, particularly given the timing of Hannah's revelation. If Hannah had been supported by the army at a time when they were attempting to raise an army, she may well have been a useful rallying point. (In 1746, the famous cross-dressing actress, Peg Woffington, was depicted in a soldier's uniform on a printed ballad entitled "The Female Volunteer: or, an attempt to make our men stand".[10]) However, there is no evidence to suggest that Hannah was used by the military in this way. In 1750, England was between wars, experiencing a rare moment of peace.

Whatever the truth, Hannah's reward of fivepence per day for the rest of her life was insufficient to live on, yet was a source of income upon which she became increasingly reliant in her later years.

10

Where do Retired Female Soldiers Go?

The final part of Robert Walker's serialised biography appeared sometime in early September 1750. Hannah was only twenty-seven years old and Walker's silence taunts us as we hunt for clues that might help expand our slender knowledge of her remaining forty years.

As a parting gesture Walker hints at Hannah's future plans, saying that she hoped to open a public house called "The Widow in Masquerade". While the majority of Hannah's chroniclers have assumed that she pursued a life in the liquor trade, there is no evidence that she ever achieved this ambition.[1]

While Hannah may have been struggling to get her business plans off the ground during this period, it seems she continued to profit from her notoriety. In 1751, with her earning ability in London diminished by her fading popularity, she took her stage act out into the provinces. There are only two advertisements plotting her movements, but hopefully further evidence of this tour will be uncovered in the future. In January 1751, dancer and manager, Jockey Adams, advertised a show at the Marchant's Hall, Broad Street, in Bristol. Part of the line-up included Hannah and her manual exercises.[2] Only a few weeks later, on 25 February, she performed for one night at the New Theatre in Bath.[3] This is the last recorded appearance she ever made in a theatre.

Following Hannah's engagement in Bath, we lose track of her for eight years. How did she earn her keep during this period? We know that by 1751 the Grays no longer inhabited Ship Street - so where did Hannah live?[4] It is possible that she returned to Worcester to visit the remnants of her family. During the heady days of mid-1750, *Berrow's Worcester Journal* clearly believed that Hannah's return to her birthplace was imminent:

> We hear that the famous Hannah Snell is expected here shortly, in order to settle in some way of life less fatiguing and dangerous than that of a military one, in which she has so bravely discharged her duty to her King and country.[5]

Two weeks later, a second report informed the newspaper's readers that

Hannah had been delayed:

> Hannah Snell, the female soldier, who has been the subject of so much conversation of late, continues singing several songs, and going thro' the manual exercise of a soldier in her regimentals, every evening at the New Wells in Goodman's Fields, London, so that the expectation of her arrival in this city (the place of her nativity) may be deferr'd.[6]

It seems that Hannah did eventually make it back to Worcestershire because a Mr Eyre of Feckenham is later reported as saying that he "remembered Hannah Snell exhibiting herself at the Talbot Inn, Bewdley, and singing a song in praise of the Duke of Cumberland".[7]

During the 1750s, Hannah settled in Newbury, Berkshire. Lying halfway between Bath and London, it is possible that she had first come to know the town on her country tour of 1751. It was in November 1759, almost a decade after the peak of her fame, that Hannah's name appeared once more in the press:

> Marriages. At Newbury, in the county of Berks, the famous Hannah Snell, who served as a marine in the last war, and was wounded at the Siege of Pondicherry, to a carpenter of that place.[8]

On 3 November Hannah married Richard Eyles in the parish church of St. Nicholas.[9] The magazine reporting on the wedding neglected to mention that while Hannah stood before the rector, Thomas Penrose, she was either heavily pregnant or her baby was being nursed somewhere among the congregation. The father is a mysterious figure, like all of Hannah's

Hannah's marriage to Richard Eyles, Newbury Marriage Register, Berks.

husbands. We know nothing more about him than that he was a carpenter and the father of Hannah's two sons. The first son, George Spence Eyles, although born in 1759, was not christened until 1765 in Chelsea and, until now, was believed to be the second child of the marriage.[10] The second son, Thomas Eyles, was christened in Newbury in 1763.[11] While the record of this birth is the only documentary evidence that we have of Thomas' existence, R.S. Kirby noted in his 1804 account of Hannah's life that "a decent provision was left by the father for the two children, but on the death of the youngest, the whole devolved to the elder brother."[12]

The 1760s was a period of grief for Hannah, with the death of both Susannah and James Gray, and possibly her husband, Richard. Whatever money Hannah made during 1750 appears not to have lasted, as all of her family died in poverty. In 1764, James Gray died of consumption at the age of sixty-one in the St. George Workhouse (only a few streets away from Ship Street).[13] Not long after, in February 1765, fifty-seven year old Susannah Gray also died of consumption in the workhouse.[14] Interestingly, Hannah's five year old son, George, had been baptised only a month earlier in Chelsea (despite the family living in Berkshire). Perhaps Hannah had just visited her ailing sister in London, or was intending to travel to Wapping after undertaking business at the Royal Hospital.

By 1772, Hannah had been widowed once more and a licence was granted for her marriage to her third husband, Richard Habgood.[15] Nothing is known of Habgood other than that he was a bachelor of the parish of Welford, Berkshire, and that he married Hannah on 16 November at Wickham Chapel.[16] There is circumstantial evidence indicating that during the 1770s Hannah left Berkshire and moved to the South Midlands, on occasions, venturing as far east as Norfolk. Whether she was living with Richard Habgood and her two sons at this time we cannot say. George Spence Eyles received sufficient education to later undertake a career as an attorney, so one assumes he was attending school during these years.

One commentator says Hannah lived in Walsall in 1775 and 1776, but has been unable to find anything to suggest why she was living there.[17] Perhaps the most extraordinary report of Hannah's activities comes from the diary of Reverend James Woodforde in 1778. For a moment it feels as if Robert Walker has taken us by the hand once more:

May 21. We all breakfasted, dined and slept again at Weston [Weston Longueville 10 miles NE of Norwich]. I walked up to the White Hart with Mr. Lewis and Bill to see a famous Woman in Men's Cloaths, by name

Hannah Snell, who was 21 years as a common soldier in the Army, and not discovered by any as a woman. Cousin Lewis has mounted guard with her abroad. She went in the Army by the name of John Gray. She has a Pension from the Crown now of 18.5.0 per annum and the liberty of wearing Men's Cloaths and also a Cockade in her hat, which she still wears. She has laid in a room with 70 Soldiers and not discovered by any of them. The forefinger of her right hand was cut of[f] by a sword at the taking of Pondicherry. She is now about 60 yrs of age and talks very sensible and well, and travels the country with Basket at her back, selling Buttons, Garters, laces etc. I took 4 Pr of 4d Buttons and gave her 0.2.6.[18]

This wonderfully embellished account of Woodforde's meeting with Hannah raises more questions than answers. Never did Walker mention Hannah losing her forefinger at Pondicherry. Was she attributing a later injury to her years as a marine? Was Hannah happy wandering the countryside, selling buttons in her male clothes and retelling her life story? Perhaps it gave her a sense of freedom, or was it nothing more than a life of poverty and hardship? Where was her family? As this meeting occurred only twelve years before Hannah entered Bedlam, it is worth noting that Woodforde says "she talks very sensible and well" and was in reasonable health at this time.

While Woodforde's diary entry gives us a snapshot of Hannah on a particular day in 1778, it provides no clue as to why, in December 1779, the *Gentleman's Magazine* incorrectly listed Hannah's death in its obituary pages:

Hannah Snell, the well-known female soldier, found dead on a heath in Warwickshire.[19]

It appeared to have been a mysterious death. Was Hannah supposed to have been murdered or was it natural causes? What was she supposed to have been doing on the heath? While Hannah lived on until 1792 it is intriguing to wonder what event may have caused this error. Was it a mistaken identity, or was Hannah found on the heath alive but under curious circumstances? Perhaps she was trying to disappear again.

In April 1780, only four months after Hannah's misreported death, George Spence Eyles, then twenty-one years old, commenced his clerkship with the King's Bench attorney, Augustine Greenland, in Marylebone.[20] This immediately raises the question of how George could afford to pay for his chosen career? It seems unlikely that Hannah would have been in much of a position to support him. In 1795, Daniel Lysons provided an enigmatic solution in his summary of Hannah's life:

A lady of fortune, who admired the heroism and eccentricity of her conduct, having honoured her with particular notice, became Godmother to her son, and contributed liberally to his education.[21]

The identity of the "lady of fortune" is unknown, but this piece of late eighteenth-century gossip provides a plausible solution to the question of George's education.

On Christmas day, 1781, George married Jane Sympson at St. Paul's, Convent Garden.[22] Hannah was not one of the official witnesses to the ceremony, but may well have been in attendance. By 1785, her health had deteriorated and George and Jane were probably caring for her, along with their two young daughters, Harriot and Elizabeth. In June of that year, the Board of Commissioners at Chelsea Hospital received a petition on Hannah's behalf requesting an increase to her pension. The board minutes note, "Hannah Snell prays addition to her pension as she is now quite infirm".[23] The Board increased Hannah's pension to a shilling a day "in compassion to her infirm state of health".[24] It is probably no coincidence that Hannah's request for an increased pension occurred just when George was due to pay one hundred pounds duty on his Articles of Clerkship, and when Jane was expecting their third child.[25]

By late 1785, Hannah had moved with her family to Stoke Newington.[26] George seemed to be constantly plagued by money problems and in December 1789, he published a portrait of Hannah to be sold by subscription.[27] It was a poor copy of an engraving originally sold in 1750 based on a portrait of Hannah by Richard Phelps, and seems a desperate attempt at reviving the career of this elderly, ailing woman.

Despite a long and colourful life, Hannah ended her days in the gloom and confinement of a cell in Bedlam. On 6 August 1791, the Hospital's Board of Governors read a petition requesting the admittance of Hannah to the asylum.[28] She was admitted on 20 August, her securities named as George Eyles, attorney, and John Day, Excise Officer.[29] The deplorable conditions in the hospital were described by a Parliamentary Committee in 1814:

Many women were locked up in their cells naked and chained, on straw, with only one blanket for a covering, and the windows being unglazed, the light in winter was shut out for the sake of warmth.[30]

Bedlam, Moorfields, around 1750.

It was under such wintry conditions that Hannah died 8 February 1792.[31] Tradition has it that she was buried in an unmarked grave at the Royal Chelsea Hospital, the ground since covered by the new infirmary.

It seems hardly surprising that even Hannah's death is touched by mystery. On 3 February, five days before her recorded death, a James Gray was buried at Chelsea Hospital.[32] It is as if the two identities of this individual had been inexplicably joined together in the same piece of earth. Perhaps the clerk recording the burial made an error and the entry should have read 13 February, although it seems unlikely that Hannah would have been buried under her pseudonym. Or maybe Hannah had simply requested that she lie with her fellow soldiers under the name that had given her a freedom experienced by few women of her time, and the name by which her shipmates had so fondly known her.

11

Who was James Gray?

What then are we to make of Hannah's story? There is little doubt that at the end of May 1750, Susannah Gray had passionately embraced a marine on her doorstep in Wapping. And while there is no question that the face that received these kisses was recognised by many as belonging to "James Gray", it is frustrating that we have nothing to prove the sex of this shadowy figure. I believe there is, however, enough circumstantial evidence with which we can make an educated guess.

I have shown that much of Robert Walker's description of Hannah's life in the marines has been based on a very intimate knowledge of Boscawen's East Indian expedition. Naval musters confirm much of Walker's intricately detailed account of the movements of "James Gray" and his/her shipmates (although in a jumbled order). Yet this information still does not provide us with an answer. We are left with two basic options - either James Gray related his adventures to his sister-in-law after returning to England, or Hannah did indeed make the journey herself.

There are at least four possible areas of investigation that may help us to reach a conclusion: the first is whether we can prove that James Gray of Ship Street was living in London at the same time that his namesake, the marine, was stationed in India; the second is to identify whether the two James Grays had different signatures; the third is to investigate whether Walker's description of Gray's life on board ship is better matched to that of a young marine of Hannah's age or of her brother-in-law, who was twenty years older; and finally, we must consider the possible mechanism by which Hannah hid her sex over such a long period of time.

Let us start with the most abstract area of investigation by examining how Hannah might have kept her secret under such difficult circumstances. I have already mentioned some of the practical methods a female soldier might employ to avoid detection, as well as the cultural factors that may have helped, but we should also consider the possibility that Hannah maintained her long-term disguise with the assistance of a fellow marine. Although the nature of this phenomenon relies on personal secrecy, female soldier and sailor biographies reveal that a surprising number of these women had an accomplice.[1]

Robert Walker mentions a number of Hannah's shipmates in the biography, but few seem an obvious choice as that of confidant. One possibility, John Hutchins, is described by Walker as "a fellow that understood himself, and behaved in somewhat a more decent manner than the rest of her shipmates", but there is no hint of intimacy between the two soldiers. The most likely candidate is Lieutenant Richard Wagget, to whom the young Gray was a servant boy between 1747 to 1749. Wagget was the man Walker described as "kindly" and Hannah's "only sincere friend", and had been cared for by Hannah when dangerously ill at Gibraltar. We know little more about him than that he had a wife and two young daughters back in England at the time of the expedition.[2] Following Wagget's death, in 1749, Hannah appears much more vulnerable to exposure in the biography and is eager to attach herself to another officer as quickly as possible. It is clear from Walker's narrative that Hannah was reliant on Wagget to help maintain her disguise, but whether this was simply her taking advantage of his senior position, or something more intimate, we may never know.

Another area of investigation, slightly less speculative, is the age gap between Hannah and her brother-in-law. Hannah was aged twenty-four in 1747 and James Gray was twenty years older. The picture Walker paints of Private Gray is that of a youth, a young man barely out of adolescence who served as a servant boy to Lieutenants Richard Wagget, William Kite and Samuel Wallis. Hannah's position as mess boy and servant is unsubstantiated and it is possible that Walker fabricated the story to give his heroine a greater credibility. However, it seems that Hannah was convincing enough as James Gray on stage that none of the marine's old acquaintances questioned her authenticity publicly. It is doubtful that there would have been such a level of acceptance if the young Hannah had been trying to impersonate her middle-aged brother-in-law.

The best evidence supporting Hannah's case will most likely come from sources that rely as little as possible on Walker's biography. The answer may well lie somewhere among the few signatures we possess of Hannah Snell and James Gray. We have one copy of Hannah's mark as it appeared in a marriage register in 1759.[3] Not surprisingly for a member of the lower classes of this period, Hannah was unable to sign her name and she marked the document with a cross. We also have James Gray's signature as it appeared on the *Eltham's* victualling accounts.[4] Again, this signature is identified only by a cross and thus similar to Hannah's mark. Unfortunately, a signature of James Gray, the carpenter, has not yet surfaced so we have not been able to see whether Hannah's brother-in-law was able to sign his name. If in the future we should discover that the male James Gray was literate enough to sign his name during the late 1740s, we will possess the strongest evidence yet that Hannah and Private Gray were one and the same person.

Perhaps the most tantalising clue lies in the eighteenth-century Land Tax Assessments held by the Guildhall library. These registers are divided up into streets within wards and list the names of the owners or occupiers of the premises within each street.[5] In 1744, James Gray first began paying taxes on a house in Ship Street. He continued making payments on the property for the next five years until, in 1751, the premises were listed as empty. Does this mean that James Gray of Ship Street was paying his taxes in person between 1747-1750 while James Gray, the marine, was in India? Such a hypothesis is highly possible, but the tax registers only required the name of the head of the household and so it is feasible that Susannah Gray paid the taxes on behalf of her husband while he was away in the East. Once again evidence that appears to support Hannah's case proves disappointingly fallible.

While I have had no qualms questioning the veracity of Hannah's earlier career as a soldier fighting against the Scots, I am less sceptical about the account of her Indian experiences between 1747-1750. Despite my rearrangement of Walker's chronology during this period, I still feel there is more evidence leaning towards Hannah than against. Until we find further material that can help determine the truth of the matter, I am prepared to say that I believe Hannah did travel to India in masquerade and, perhaps more importantly, this was a view held by many of her contemporaries.

Are these the mark of the same person? While the two crosses appear unalike, it is clear from marines' accounts kept on the Eltham that James Gray and his mates signed their cross differently each time.

Afterword

Irrespective of what the truth about Hannah may have been, the story of her adventures has taken on a life of its own. Over the last 250 years her name has been appropriated by many different people and has served a variety of purposes. Interest in Hannah's life has been cyclical - during some decades her story was barely mentioned, and in others it became a focal point of interest and discussion. This pattern not only measures the rediscovery of Hannah by succeeding generations, but also marks significant moments in history (such as those associated with the quest for women's rights) in which Hannah's story is given a new relevancy.

Following the initial burst of publicity in 1750, there was little mention of Hannah other than a reference to her marriage in 1759, her prematurely reported death in 1779, and the reprinting of her biography as a chapbook. Hannah's illness and death, in 1792, prompted the odd comment in books and periodicals but surprisingly little reaction.

Despite Hannah's death, early accounts continued to relay contemporary gossip. In 1795 Daniel Lysons mentions "The Lady of Fortune", in 1804 R.S. Kirby reports one source saying Hannah's secret was actually revealed in India, and a Dr Prattinton says that in 1826 he was told that Hannah's son "married a woman who sold smuggled laces in the Haymarket". In 1872 Charles Dickens' periodical *All the Year Round* retold Hannah's story in an article examining "British Amazons". Up until the final quarter of the 1800s, reports about Hannah remained minimal.

From the late 1870s there appears to have been a growing interest in Hannah, peaking in the 1890s. By this time, the story had become fixed because all of Hannah's contemporaries were long since dead. During a period of rising feminism and the suffragettes, there was a great deal of interest in female soldiers generally, and Hannah's story appeared in accounts entitled *Female Warriors, British Amazons, Eighteenth-Century Amazons, and Women Adventurers*. In the 1880s and 1890s *Notes and Queries* published a series of letters about female soldiers - many of them concentrating on Hannah.

Undoubtedly, the most significant moment in the telling of Hannah's story occurred in 1898 with the publication of the *Dictionary of National Biography*. The information and attitudes contained within the DNB's entry on Hannah were to be repeated throughout the following century.

The new century saw a decline in interest in Hannah which did not really return until the early 1970s. In 1909, Hannah appeared as a character in *A Pageant of Great Women,* a play by Cicely Hamilton, presented by the Women Writers' Suffrage League. The following year, Bram Stoker wrote his own version of her life in *Famous Imposters.* In 1927, the Prime Minister, Stanley Baldwin, prompted a number of newspaper articles about Hannah when he retold the story at the inaugural Worcestershire Association banquet. There were few accounts between the 1930s and the 1960s. In 1966 John Laffin published *Women in Battle* and further reports appeared in 1971 and 1973.

In 1974 there was a dramatic shift in the way in which Hannah's story was told and in some ways reminiscent of accounts appearing in the 1890s and early 1900s. The Worcester Repertory Company presented a rock opera, *The Scurrilous Adventures of Hannah Snell* - the internal contradictions within the work epitomising the community's struggle with the women's liberation movement. In 1975 Hannah featured in the *Guinness Guide to Feminine Achievements.*

Since the early 1970s, there has been a steady coverage of Hannah's story in newspapers, encyclopedias and many other books. In 1988, Shirley Gee's radio play inspired by Hannah's life, *Against the Wind,* was broadcast, and in 1989 the first edition of Walker's biography was reprinted in America.

Yet another shift in the treatment of Hannah's life has occurred over the last decade, driven by the growing interest in the study of the construction of gender and sexuality. In 1989 appeared both Julie Wheelwright's *Amazons and Military Maids* and Dekker and Van de Pol's *The Tradition of Female Transvestism in Early Modern Europe,* and in 1996, Suzanne J. Stark's *Female Tars* was released.

While there have been many different approaches to Hannah's life - from the pens of journalists, playwrights, and academics - there has never been a biography on which people can safely rely. Coupled with the collection held by the Royal Marines Museum, Southsea, I hope my own reappraisal will provide new avenues of interest and exploration for those wishing to continue to work on this extraordinary story.

Notes

Guide To References and Abbreviations

SM: Public Record Office (PRO). ADM 36/3472, Swallow Musters.
SCL: PRO. ADM 51/917, Swallow Captain's Log, 1745-1749.
EM: PRO. ADM 36/1033, Eltham Musters.
ECL: PRO. ADM 51/309, Eltham Captain's Log, 1743-1750.
SWL: National Maritime Museum. HMS Eltham ADM/L/E/95, Eltham Lieutenant's Logs 1748-1750, Samuel Wallis' log.

Introduction (pp. 9-11)

1. From an unknown publication. 14 September 1791. Cutting found in Add. Man. 5723 Biographical Adversaria. British Library.
2. Walker Biography: *The Female Soldier; or The Surprising Life and Adventures of Hannah Snell*, The Corner of Elliot's Court, in the Little Old Bailey, 1750. 1st edition released in July, 42pp. 2nd edition was released in 9 parts between July and September, 187pp. All references refer to the 2nd edition unless otherwise cited. Although the author of the biography is unknown, Walker was closely involved in its production and may well have been the author. For convenience I have identified Walker as the creator.
3. The earliest questioning is found in R.S. Kirby's *Kirby's Wonderful or Scientific Museum...*, London, 1804, Vol II, p. 430. Later discussions in *Notes and Queries*, 8th S. II. July 30, '92, p. 88; 8th S. II. Aug. 27,'92, p. 171; 8th S. II. Dec. 3,'92, p. 455; 8th S. III. Jan. 28, '93, p. 77.
4. See Dianne Dugaw's introduction to *The Female Soldier; or, The Surprising Adventures of Hannah Snell* (1st edition), The Augustan Reprint Society, publ. no. 257, Los Angeles, 1989. Also see Dianne Dugaw, *Warrior Women and Popular Balladry*, 1650-1850, C.U.P., Cambridge, 1989.

Worcester (pp. 12-14)

1. Daniel Defoe, *A Tour thro' the Whole Island of Great Britain*, 1724-26, Vol.11, pp. 442-445. Reprinted by Frank Cass & Co. Ltd, London, 1968.
2. Worcester Record Office. BA2036/21b, Marriage Bond and Allegation, 2 December 1702 - marriage of Samuel Snell, dyer, aged 22 and Elizabeth Marston, 'aged about 20'. Fortunately, Snell was an uncommon name in Worcestershire at this time.
3. Leases show that Samuel Snell was living in one of a row of houses numbered 17-25 Friar Street. No. 25 has been suggested as the most likely candidate. See Pat Hughes & Nicholas Molyneux, *Worcester Streets - Friar Street*, Self-published, Worcester, 1994, p. 11.
4. Worcester Record Office. BA2036/28a, Marriage Bond and Allegation, 30 June 1709 - marriage of Samuel Snell, widower, aged 29 years and Mary Williams, aged 25.
5. David Whitehead, *Urban Renewal and Suburban Growth; The Shaping of Georgian Worcester*, Worcestershire Historical Society, Occasional Publication No. 5, 1989, pp. 2-3.
6. Isaac Watts, 1728, quoted by Bridget Hill in *Eighteenth Century Women; An Anthology*, Allen & Unwin, London, 1987, p. 66.

The Call of the City (pp. 15-17)

1. Inexplicably, Land Tax Assessments for Wapping show that James Gray first began paying taxes for Ship Street in 1744, four years after Walker says Hannah arrived there [Guildhall Library MS6016/1630].
2. There is no record of the marriage in extant Fleet registers.
3. Anon, *The Life and Adventures of Mrs Christian Davies, commonly called Mother Ross...*, R. Montagu, London, 1740. Reprinted in *The Novels and Miscellaneous Works of Daniel Defoe*, Thomas Tegg, Oxford, Vol. VIII, 1840, p. 257.

Rebellion (pp. 18-21)

1. *London Gazette*, 23 November 1745.
2. A George Francis Beck of Feckenham (near Worcester) was baptised on 5 May, 1720 (International Genealogical Index). There are no Guise musters extant to confirm Beck's enlistment at Carlisle.
3. Coventry Record Office. 346/23, Council Meeting Minutes, 1727/8.
4. In 1746, Walker published a biography of Lord Lovatt, which mentions Captain Miller. It is also likely that he knew Coventry through his newspaper interests in the Birmingham region.
5. Charles Lethbridge Kingsford, *The Story of the Royal Warwickshire Regt..,* County Life, 1921, p. 33.
6. J.M Kitzmiller, *In Search of the "Forlorn Hope"; a Comprehensive Guide to Locating British Regiments and their Whereabouts,* Manuscript Pub. Foundation, Salt Lake City, 1988, Section V, p. 260.
7. A letter signed by 'M.' in *Notes and Queries,* 8th S. II. Dec. 3, '92, p. 455.

A Passage to India (pp. 22-24)

1. SCL: Entry for the 24/10/1747. (The naval day ran from midday to midday. I have adjusted all dates in the main text to a standard civilian day.)
2. SM: (October - December 1747) Lists the new recruits originating from Portsmouth as: Rich. Wagget, Geo. Johnsone, Jas. Chad, Robt. Coventry, Jn. Hutchins, Dougal McDougal and James Gray.
3. Brigitte Eriksson (ed.), quoted by Rudolf M. Dekker and Lotte C. Van de Pol in *The Tradition of Female Transvestism in Early Modern Europe,* Macmillan, London, 1989, p.16.
4. Suzanne J. Stark, *Female Tars; Women Aboard Ship in the Age of Sail,* Constable, London, 1996, pp. 89-90.
5. For Rowzier's account of the storm see PRO. ADM 1/2382, Letter 3, Captain's Letters, Rowzier.
6. Walker says that while at Madeira, the *Swallow* took on some extra men from the *Sheerness* Privateer (p. 37). Rowzier verifies this in his log, but also notes that the majority of new recruits actually came from the prison on the island [SCL: 26-27 February, 1747].
7. PRO. ADM 1/160, Boscawen's Letters to the Admiralty, p. 273.
8. PRO. ADM 1/160, Boscawen's Letters to the Admiralty, Results of Council of War, pp. 297-299.

The Siege of Pondicherry (pp. 25-28)

1. PRO. ADM 1/160, Griffin's Letters to the Admiralty, p. 61.
2. On a journey to the Pacific (1766-69), Jeanne Baré successfully disguised herself as a man while on ship. However, upon her arrival at Tahiti, her true sex was recognised by the native Tahitians the moment she stepped on shore. See Stark, p. 91.
3. Royal Archives, Windsor Castle. The Cumberland papers, Box 62/C3, Major Mompesson's Orders for the Pondicherry Siege. See orders for 6 August, 1748.
4. Both Robert Orme and Lord Clive were critical of the poor handling of the siege. See Robert Orme, *A History of the Military Transaction of the British Nation in Indostan....,* Lond., 1763-1778, Vol. I, p. 110. Also see Clive's comments in India Office Library, Orme MSS, India Vol. I, pp. 111-120.
5. The diary of James Miller, 1745-50, was reprinted in *The Journal of the Society of Army Historical Research,* October 1924, Vol. III, No. 14.
6. The transfer is mentioned in the *Eltham's* 1st lieut.'s log on 9 October, 1748, in the SCL on 11 October, as well as the respective musters for each ship during this period [see SM and EM].

The Mystery of Hannah's Wounds (pp. 29-33)

1. Walker's vagueness about chronology during this period is particularly noticeable because for most of the 2nd edition he is very specific about when events occurred.
2. Walker says the *Eltham* left on 19 November, but EM, ECL, & SWL show that she left a month earlier, on 19 October 1749. This is probably due to a memory or clerical error rather than a time-shift.
3. The only detailed account of the siege was made by Clive of India [India Office Library, Orme MSS, India Vol. I, pp. 219-225]. While his description is graphic, he does not mention how the marines were involved in the battle.
4. William Belchier (or Belsches) was surgeon of the Naval Hospital at Fort St. David, and agent for the

squadron. [Love, Henry Davison. *Vestiges of Old Madras.* Vol.II. p. 386].

5. ADM 36/4183, *Tartar* Musters 1749/50.

6. Dekker and Van de Pol cite the example of one particular female soldier: "Nursing and medical treatments could involve disrobing, although, as the story of Maritgen Jans shows, the standards of hygiene at the time were rather low. The 'Stout-Hearted Heroine' relates how she was wounded in the backside in battle, but was nonetheless successful in keeping her real sex hidden throughout the two months of nursing. When gangrene threatened, however, the surgeon brought in another doctor to cut out the wound. 'To that end, and being completely bared by the manservants, the doctor who had been called in saw what I had then so long hidden. 'A pox to say it', he said to the doctor, 'but there is one cut more than we thought to find'". p. 21.

7. EM: July - August, 1749. While it was common for ships to unload their sick when they arrived at port, and these 20 sick came from a contingent of 234 crew, the numbers during August and September were much higher than previous months and at similar levels to those during the Siege of Pondicherry.

Homeward Bound (pp. 34-36)

1. SWL: entry for 19 October 1749.

2. SWL: entry for 20 October 1749: "At 6am Departed this Life Mr Richard Wagget Lieut. of Marines in Cockarens Regiment". Hannah left England on the *Swallow* in the company of 21 marines, of whom only 13 returned alive.

3. A "Molly" was slang for a male homosexual. See Alan Bray's *Homosexuality in Renaissance England*, Gay Men's Press, London, 1982.

4. It is difficult to ascertain whether Summs did actually die in Genoa. It is uncertain as to what name he would have used and the records of the time appear incomplete - there are only two death sentences recorded between 1746-47. Curiously, the way in which Summs was said to have died was not an official punishment. At this time criminals were either decapitated or hanged, only pirates being drowned. It is possible that his death was a revenge killing or that the entire story is a fabrication.

5. SWL: Walker says the *Eltham* left on 3 May.

6. EM. Walker says that the *Eltham* arrived at Portsmouth on 1 June. While much of Walker's description of Hannah's first weeks in England has been factually verified, his chronology for this period is dated exactly a week later than actually occurred. As the biography was written less than a month after Hannah's arrival in England, the error seems a curious lapse of memory. In effect, those reading the biography were unaware that Hannah had spent an extra week in England prior to her revelation. Did Walker and Hannah need this extra week to prepare their story properly?

7. PRO. ADM 96/129, effective and subsistence lists and musters. John Greenway paid five shillings subsistence money to each of Frazier's marines who "Landed from his Mjy. Ship *Eltham* 25 inst. in the Evening from Portsmouth to London". Those paid were: Robert Richardson, Robert Brown, John Bulchings, George Hurley, Edward Jefferys, John Hurley, Andrew Gray, James Gray, Thomas Meredith and Dougal McDougal

Fame (pp. 37-43)

1. Walker says it was Saturday, 9 June. However, there is a Marine's account showing that Gray was paid 1.18.3$^1/_2$ seapay by Winter on 2 June [PRO. ADM 96/129, Marine's Registers - effective and subsistive lists and musters, 1739-1755].

2. We have no record of the contents within this petition. However, in the 1st edition of the biography Walker writes "a petition was drawn up, setting forth her adventures, and the hardships she underwent together with the many wounds she received". In the second edition Walker identifies the wounds specifically as "the wounds she had received at the siege of Pondicherry". We can actually see Walker formulating his story through his changes to the 2nd edition.

3. *Whitehall Evening Post or, London Intelligencer.* Saturday June 23, to Tues June 26 1750.

4. For more information about Walker see *Serial Publication in England before 1750* by R.M. Wiles, Cambridge at the University Press, 1957.

5. In both the 1st and 2nd editions of the biography, a copy of the affidavit follows the title page. The document was often used by Walker in his advertisements for the biography.

6. The advertisement appeared in the *Whitehall Evening Post, The London Evening Post,* and the *Penny London Post.* It began appearing in *The General Advertiser* on 29 June.

7. The first part was advertised as "published this day" in *The Ladies Magazine,* 14 July 1750.

8. I have found advertisements for the biography covering 28 June - 11 August 1750, in *The Whitehall Evening Post, The Penny London Post, The London Evening Post, The General Advertiser, The Ladies Magazine, The Cambridge Journal,* and *Berrow's Worcester Journal.*

9. Known engravings of Hannah sold in 1750 were catalogued by Henry Bromley in 1793. There are at least another two engravings that were not listed: an illustration of Hannah in a marine uniform taken from her stage performances by F. Johnson, and a series of four pictures illustrating Hannah's manual exercises (see p. 42) - one of which was reproduced in a Dutch edition of the biography in 1750.

10. *The Whitehall and General Evening Post,* 30 June. Reproduced in *The Derby Mercury,* June 29 to July 6, 1750 p. 3.

11. An indication of what some audiences may have expected is evident in the illustration accompanying the text of the "New Song" sold at the Wells' bar during Hannah's performances. It is a violent image of a pirate woman holding a cutlass in one hand and an axe in the other. This was certainly not the image portrayed by Hannah on stage.

12. A daily ad for Hannah's performances was placed in *The General Advertiser* throughout the season.

13. On 25 August *The General Advertiser* carried an Advertisement noting that Hannah would "sing the new song of the herring-fishery, as it was sung by the anti-Gallicans at Draper's Hall".

14. There has been much confusion about where Hannah performed. All the theatres connected to Hannah's name are in some way associated with the word "wells". Hannah definitely appeared at the New Wells, Goodman's Fields and the New Wells Spa, Clerkenwell, but these are probably the only London theatres in which she performed. Both Sadler's Wells and the Royalty Theatre, Wellclose Square (not built until 1787) have been cited as possible venues but with no supporting evidence.

A Question of Money (pp. 44-46)

1. Walker biography, 1st edition, p. 40. When discussing the Cumberland pension, Walker notes "it is not doubted but his Royal Highness will make some handsome allowance, exclusive of Chelsea College, to which she is entitled".

2. *Penny London Post,* June 27 to June 29, 1750, p. 2.

3. The papers of William Augustus, Duke of Cumberland, Royal Archives, Windsor Castle.

4. This delivery of the certificate was reported in *The Derby Mercury,* June 29 to July 6 and attributed to the *Whitehall and General Evening Post,* 30 June.

5. An out pensioner was a wounded ex-soldier who was paid a pension, but did not live at the Hospital.

6. WO 116/4, Chelsea Hospital admission book, 1746-54.

7. WO 250/471, Chelsea Hospital board minutes, 1743-54 & WO 250/374, Abstracts from selected board minutes, 1745-1825.

8. Preface to the 1840 edition of *The Life and Adventures of Mrs Christian Davies...*

9. There is no doubt that the documents needed to authenticate the story were available by mid-June. The Admiralty had obtained many of the lieutenants' logs by then. It also appears that William Belchier's Cuddelore Hospital accounts had been received by the Commissioners of the Sick and Hurt Board by this time [Dispatches from England Vol. LIII-LVI PR/CH 1749-53. See volume LIV pp. 57-59].

10. Dugaw, Dianne. *Warrior Women,* p. 53

Where do Retired Female Soldiers Go? (pp. 47-52)

1. I have found no evidence of Hannah's pub. This has been confirmed by Suzanne Stark, p. 107.

2. Fidelis Morgan, *The Well-Known Trouble Maker. A life of Charlotte Charke,* Faber and Faber, 1988, p. 152

3. *The Bath Journal,* 25 February 1750-51.

4. Land Tax Assessments. In 1751 under Ship Street, the entry reads: James Gray - empty.

5. *Berrow's Worcester Journal*, 19 July 1750.

6. *Berrow's Worcester Journal*, 2 August 1750.

7. Bound into the Worcester Public Library's edition of Walker's biography are the hand written notes of R.R. Duke, dated 1885. He says that Eyre's recollections of Hannah are from the M.S. collection for a history of the county by a Dr Prattinton.

8. *The Universal Chronicle*, Nov 3/10, 1759, p. 359, col.3.

9. Berkshire Record Office. Newbury Marriage Register, November 1759 [D/P 89 1/11].

10. St. Luke, Chelsea, baptism register: 1765 17 January, George Spence son of Richard Eyles and Hannah. George Eyles was at least 21 years old when he married by Banns in 1781. Ratcliffe Workhouse records show that he was 85 years old in 1844, and his 1844 burial record also confirms this.

11. St. Nicholas, Newbury, baptism register: 1763, 13 Mar., Thomas son of Richard and Hannah Eyles.

12. R.S. Kirby, p. 438.

13. St.George-in-the-East burials: 1764, 7 Mar., James Gray, Workhouse, died of consumption, age 61.

14. St.George-in-the-East burials: 1765, 20 Feb., Susannah Gray, W.H., died of consumption, age 57.

15. Wilts Record Office. Marriage Licences, 12 November 1772.

16. Berks Record Office. D/P 147 1/4, Welford Parish marriage register, 16 November 1772.

17. E.G. O'Donoghue, *The Story of Bethlehem Hospital from its Foundation in 1247...*, T. Fisher Unwin, London,1914, note for p. 278, line 30: "It appears from records in Chelsea Hospital for 1775-1776 that Hannah Snell was resident for some years at Walsall in Staffordshire, but the town clerk has been unable to trace any account of her residence".

18. John Beresford (ed.), *Passages from the five Volumes of the Diary of a Country Parson, 1758-1802. The Reverend James Woodforde*, O.U.P, London, 1935, p. 118.

19. *Gentleman's Magazine*, December 1779, Vol. 49, p. 616.

20. PRO. KB 105/1 4254, Affidavits of Due Execution of Articles.

21. Daniel Lysons, *The Environs of London being an Historical Account of the Towns, Villages and the Hamlets within Twelve Miles of That Capital*, London, Vol. II, p. 164.

22. Victoria Library, Westminster. St. Paul, Convent Garden, Marriage Register, 25 December 1781.

23. PRO. WO 250/477, Chelsea Hospital Board Minutes, 9 June 1785.

24. PRO. WO 250/463, Chelsea Hospital Journal, 9 June, 1785.

25. Hannah's eighteen pound pension would have been paid in a lump sum in June of each year. By the terms of his clerkship contract, George would have finished on 29 April, but his contract was not read in court until 28 November [PRO, KB 105/1 4254]. Their daughter, Jane, was baptised in September.

26. PRO. IND 1/4583, Articles of Clerkship, Kings Bench. George gives his address as Stoke Newington. The earliest account to mention George by name was *Robinson's History of Stoke Newington*, 1820, in which the author says Hannah lived with George in Church Street, Stoke Newington.

27. In 1804, R.S. Kirby wrote: '[the funds left by his father] proving inadequate to the support of a large family, he some years since published by subscription, a portrait of his mother, underneath which were a few particulars of her history'.

28. Bethlem Royal Hospital Archives, Weekly Committee books.

29. Bethlem Royal Hospital Archives. Admission Register.

30. J.C. Platt, 'Medical and Surgical Hospitals and Lunatic Asylums', in Charles Knight (ed.), *London*, London, 1843, p. 383.

31. Bethlem Royal Hospital Archives. Noted in the Admission Register as well as the Weekly Committee book for the 11 February.

32. PRO. RG4/4330, Registers of burials, Royal Chelsea Hospital, 1691-1856.

Who was James Gray? (pp. 53-55)

1. Women whose secret was known by others include: Christian Davies, Anne Talbot, Emma Edmonds, Loreta Valesquez, and Princess Kati Dadeshkeliani. See Julie Wheelwright's *Amazons and Military Maids*, Pandora Press, London, 1989.

2. Richard Wagget's will reveals that he left a wife, Anne, and two daughters, Anne and Elizabeth [PRO. Prob II/780]

3. St Nicholas' Parish Marr. Register, 3 November 1759, p. 44. [Berks Record Office. D/P 89 1/11].

4. PRO. ADM 96/129, Marines' Registers - effective and subsistive lists and musters, 1739-1755.

5. Guildhall Library. MS6016/1630, Land Tax Assessments, Tower Division - 1744 to 1750, Parish of St. George-in-the-East.